LEARNING
about
NATURE
through
INDOOR
GARDENING

by **Virginia W. Musselman**

STACKPOLE BOOKS

LEARNING ABOUT NATURE THROUGH
INDOOR GARDENING

Copyright © 1972 by
THE STACKPOLE COMPANY
Published by
STACKPOLE BOOKS
Cameron and Kelker Streets
Harrisburg, Pa. 17105

Price: $3.95

Printed in U.S.A.

Library of Congress Cataloging in Publication Data

Musselman, Virginia W
    Learning about nature through indoor gardening.

    Bibliography: p.
    1. House plants. 2. Nature study. I. Title.
II. Title: Indoor gardening.
SB419.M985   635.96'5   75-179606
ISBN 0-8117-0945-0

For
Travis Poillon,
who has a green thumb for living

Contents

Introduction   /11

Handy reference guide to familiar
plants, complete with common and
botanical names and where to find them
in this book.

**Guide to Plants
for Indoor Gardening**   /14

Simple definitions for the thirty-five
most frequently used indoor
gardening terms.

Glossary   /17

PART I   **LEARNING
ABOUT
PLANTS**

All about seeds, cells, roots,
stems, leaves, buds, flowers,
and life cycles.

**How Plants
Grow**   /22

General how-to's on seeding, transplanting, cutting, and layering. Learning about basic care of plants.

How to Grow Plants /31

How to recognize, deal with, and prevent some of the most common plant diseases and pests. Safety tips for using pesticides.

About Plant Diseases and Pests /40

PART II INDOOR GARDENING GALORE

Considering common fruits and vegetables, where they come from, and how they grow . . . using everything from apples and coffee beans to pineapples and sweet potatoes!

Gardening Fun with Kitchen Throw-aways /46

Growing and using nine historic herbs for fancy flavors!

Raising Exotic Herbs for Cooking Use /55

Crocus, narcissus, hyacinth—dealing with all the favorites. "Bulbs-in-a-sponge" and three other exciting bulb ideas.

Care and Culture of Blooming Bulbs /62

Where to place and how to care for azaleas, chrysanthemums, Easter lilies, and a dozen other gift plants.

Looking Gift Plants in the Pot /72

Beautiful foliage plants; how to choose and place them, and how to give them the special care they so deserve.

Living Room Foliage: Tropical Plants in the Home /84

Learning to recognize, grow, and care for such favorites as African violets, geraniums, begonias, and half a dozen more.

Enjoying Flower Power at Its Brightest /99

Supporting and leading thirteen different varieties of those clinging, climbing, twisting indoor vines.

Clingers, Climbers, and Twisters: The Ivy League /110

Imaginative ideas for extending your gardening. Everything from flower arranging to mini-greenhouses to growing your own Christmas tree!

Exciting Do-togethers for Enthusiastic Indoor Gardeners /116

Where to get seeds, plants, herbs, and books to aid in exploring indoor gardening.

Resources /124

9

Introduction

This is the fourth book in a series on learning about nature through special activities, including games, crafts, pets, and now indoor gardening. It is designed to help parents, grandparents, teachers, youth leaders, and other adults to use the acts of growing and caring for plants as a way to arouse the child's interest and to help him to discover for himself that without plants, life on this planet Earth would not be possible.

No young child can be expected to grasp the broad principles of ecology. He can, however, make his first encounter with the miracle of watching a tiny seed sprout roots and grow leaves. He can experience for the first time the excitement of watching a bulb grow in water, using its own stored food supply to produce flowers. He can discover for himself how everyday foods like peas and beans are really seeds, and he can plant them to prove it. He can find out that a big avocado seed will grow into a tall, tree-like plant, and learn that avocados do not come just from a supermarket. He can find out, by growing one, what a pineapple plant looks like, and that small pineapples grow on the plant.

On a small scale in his own home, schoolroom, or youth center, at his own pace, the child can experience the miracle of plant life and growth. He can discover that plants, like pets, are living, breathing organisms, with their own special needs and habits of growth. He can learn their names and how to recognize them by their colors, leaves, fragrance, and way of growing. Like pets, too, they will respond to his tender loving care.

He can find out for himself that growing a plant requires effort and patience on his part. As Kipling put it, "Gardens are not made by saying 'Oh, how pretty' and sitting in the shade."

The city child living in a high-rise apartment house has only limited contact with plants outdoors. Parks are few and often far away. Trees are scarce and too tall for intimate study. Outdoor gardens, where there are any, are full of "Don't touch" signs. For the child who lives in the suburbs or in some area where an outdoor garden is possible, it is likely to be dominated by very busy adults with little time for encouraging youthful efforts. While outdoor gardening by the child may be difficult to provide, indoor gardening is easily possible, whether in the heart of the city, in the suburbs, or in rural areas. Homes need plants wherever they may be.

Indoors at the kitchen table or other informal area, the child and adult can "mess around" with seeds, cuttings, pots, sand, peat moss, soil, and plants. With just a little ingenuity, effort, and imagination, indoor gardening can be made the most rewarding and interesting of hobbies that can be shared by child and adult. Growing indoor plants has become so popular that supplies are easy to find. Today most supermarkets provide a section of plant supplies. Many shopping malls have a garden center. Florist shops sell supplies as well as plants. Plant nurseries have local outlets. Chain stores and "five and dime" stores carry potting soil, peat or sphagnum moss, humus, sand, pebbles, plant sprays, pots, and other supplies. The pet sections in stores often are possibilities for sand, pebbles, pearlite, and vermiculite. Go looking for supplies together.

In the city apartment without a terrace, or in a suburban or rural home without a patio or porch, ingenuity and forethought can solve many problems. A dark closet can substitute for a cold, dark place for bulbs to "rest". A cold bedroom can be used to grow those bulbs and other plants that dislike heat. A curtained window can provide light shade for the plants that cannot stand direct sun. Lamps and fluorescent lights permit plants to grow in dark corners or on top of chests or bookcases.

With a little planning, the child and adult can watch and foster the life cycle of a plant from seed to seed-making. Together they can see new leaves unfold, flowers bud and blossom, and seeds develop for new plants. They can learn and practice other ways of plant propagation. They can find out that plants have rest periods, that some plants die after seedbearing, that some make growth one year and seeds the next, and that some plants live and bloom for many years.

Sharing a hobby is a most binding experience for a child and adult. It is best carried out by working together in active participation, experimenting and talking about what happens. The adult must be willing to take the time to help the child when needed, share the care of plants, talk about plant origins, discuss the ways in which herbs are used, how vegetables grow, which plants have lovely flowers, which are grown for their foliage.

It is not wise to try to do too much too fast. Children, like plants, develop at their own rate. Growing one small plant may be enough at one time to satisfy a child's interest. But always there should be provision for learning *more*. The doors to learning about nature should never close.

Guide to Plants for Indoor Gardening

Name	Botanical Name	Page
African violet	*Saintpaulia* species	35, 43, 100-102
Amaryllis	*Hippiastrum equestri*	69-70
Arrowhead	*Syngonium* or *Nephthytis*	87-88
Artillery Plant	*Pilea microphylla*	88
Aspidistra	*Aspidistra elatior*	88
Avocado	*Persea americana*	48-50
Azalea	*Rhododendron* species	75-76, 122
Baby's Tears	*Helxine soleirolii*	88
Basil	*Ocimum basilicum*	55, 56, 57, 58
Begonia	*Begonia* species	34, 36, 102-103
Blackeyed Susan	*Thunbergia alata*	112
Bromeliad	Bromeliaceae	53-54, 103-104
Cactus	Cactaceae	74, 86, 99, 104-105
Caladium	*Caladium bicolor*	85, 88-89
Chinese Evergreen	*Aglaonema modestum*	89
Chives	*Allium schoenoprasum*	55, 56, 59
Christmas Pepper	*Capsicum frutescens*	77
Chrysanthemum	*Chrysanthemum* species	77-78

Name	Botanical Name	Page
Cineraria	*Senecio cruentus*	78
Citrus	*Citrus* species	51-52, 78-79
Coleus	*Coleus blumei*	34, 90
Columnea	*Columnea* species	112
Crocus	*Crocus* species	64, 67, 70-71
Cyclamen	*Cyclamen indicum*	42, 64, 79
Daffodils	*Narcissus* species	71, 76
Dieffenbachia	*Dieffenbachia pictum*	37, 90-91
Dragon Plant	*Dracaena draco*	38, 91
Easter Lily	*Lilium longiflorum* var. eximium	79-80
English Ivy	*Hedera helix*	110, 112
Fiddleleaf Fig	*Ficus lyrata*	91
Freesias	*Freesia refracta, armstrongii*	64
Gardenia	*Gardenia jasminoides*	80
Geranium	*Pelargonium* species	34, 105-107, 111
Gloxinia	*Sinningia speciosa*	80, 107
Grape Ivy	*Cissus rhombifolia*	112-113
Hyacinth	*Hyacinthus orientalis*	64, 65-67, 70-71, 76
Hydrangea	*Hydrangea macrophylla*	80, 81
Indoor Oak	*Nicodemia diversifolia*	113
Jerusalem Cherry	*Solanum pseudo-capsicum*	81
Jonquils	*Narcissus jonquilla*	64-65
Kalanchoe	*Kalanchoe blossfeldiana*	36, 81-82
Kangaroo Vine	*Cissus antarctica*	114
Lantana	*Lantana camara*	34, 111
Lily of the Valley	*Convallaria majalis*	67-68
Madagascar Jasmine	*Stephanotis floribunda*	114
Marjoram	*Majorana hortensis*	55, 56, 59
Narcissus	*Narcissus* species	63, 64-65, 76
Norfolk Island Pine	*Araucaria excelsa*	91
Orchid Cactus	*Epiphyllum* species	114-115
Palm	Palmaceae	91
Parsley	*Petroselinum hortense*	47, 56, 57, 59
Passion Flower	*Passiflora* species	115
Pellionia	*Pellionia daveauana, pulchra*	115

Name	Botanical Name	Page
Peperomia	*Peperomia* species	91, 94
Philodendron	*Philodendron* species	34, 94, 115
Piggyback Plant	*Tolmiea menziesii*	94-95
Pittosporum	*Pittosporum tobira*	95-96
Podocarpus	*Podocarpus macrophylla*	96
Poinsettia	*Euphorbia pulcherrima*	35, 82-83, 121, 122
Prayer Plant	*Maranta leuconeura* var. kerchoveana	96
Rose	*Rosa* species	36, 107-108, 111
Rosemary	*Rosmarinus officinalis*	55, 56, 59-60
Rubber Plant	*Ficus elastica, decora*	38, 96
Sage	*Salvia officinalis*	55, 56, 57, 60
Scilla	*Scilla* species	64, 68
Shrimp Plant	*Beloperone guttata*	35, 108
Snake Plant	*Sansevieria thyrsiflora*	36, 97-98
Snowdrop Plant	*Galanthus nivalis*	64
Spider Plant	*Anthericum liliago*	98
Sultana	*Impatiens sultana, holstii*	109
Tarragon	*Artemisia dracunculus*	56, 60-61
Ti Plant	*Cordyline terminalis*	98
Umbrella Plant	*Schefflera actinophylla*	38, 98
Wax Plant	*Hoya carnosa*	115

Glossary

ANNUAL   A plant that blooms, sets seeds, and dies in the same year.

ANTHER   The part of a stamen that develops and contains pollen. Pollen sac.

AXIL   Upper angle made by the stem of a leaf and the stem of the plant.

BIENNIAL   A plant that grows foliage in one year, and flowers and sets seed in the next year.

BLADE   The expanded part of a leaf or petal.

BRACT   Modified leaf, sometimes colored, like the red or white "petals" of poinsettia.

BULB   A thickened bud, usually underground, capable of producing a new plant. Also applied to tuber and corm.

CALYX   The external, usually green or leafy part of a flower. The outer circle of sepals.

CARPEL   A simple pistil or one member of a compound pistil.

CORM   Short, bulb-like, underground, upright stem, invested with a few thin membranes or scale leaves, as in crocus and gladiola.

COROLLA   The ring of petals of a bloom, usually colorful.

CROCKS   Broken pieces of clay flowerpots used in bottom of pots to provide drainage.

CUTTING   A piece of a plant cut off and used to produce a new plant.

DORMANT   Resting, inactive.

FRUIT   Part of the plant that holds the seed. Can be small seedpods or large, like grapefruit.

HERB   A non-woody plant which lies naturally to the ground.

HORMONE   A chemical product that produces growth activity in a living organism such as a plant.

INFLORESCENCE   A collection of very small flowers around a central stalk or stem, such as the flower spike of the Bromeliad plant family, of which the pineapple is a member, or in certain trees, such as the horse chestnut.

LAYERING   Propagating a plant by bending a living shoot down to the ground so that it will strike root and become another plant like the parent plant.

LEAF   Lateral outgrowth of the stem of a plant.

NODE   The place on a stem from which a bud or leaf grows.

OVULE   A body in the ovary of the pistil containing the egg which, after fertilization, becomes the seed.

PERENNIAL   A plant that lasts year after year, usually blooming and setting seed each year.

PERIANTH   A combined calyx and corolla of a flower when so alike they are indistinguishable.

PETIOLE   The stalk that supports the leaf.

PIP   Dormant root of certain plants such as lily of the valley and anemone. The seed of the apple.

PISTIL   Female part of a flower consisting of an ovary with its appendages. Seedbearing organ, which remains when petals are gone.

SEPAL   A leaf-like division of the calyx.

SETS   Small, immature onions produced by close seeding one season, and used in place of seeds the next season.

SLIP   A cutting used to propagate a plant.

SPORES   Asexual reproductive bodies produced by non-flowering plants, usually one-celled and different from seeds in that they contain no embryos. Some plant diseases are spread by spores.

STAMEN   Male part of a flower made up of anther and filament.

STIGMA   Tip of the pistil which receives the pollen.

STOMATA   Pores on leaves, invisible to the naked eye.

VEIN   A fine vessel which conducts water and makes the skeleton of the leaf.

Part
I

LEARNING
ABOUT
PLANTS

CHAPTER 1

How Plants Grow

Plants are like pets. They grow and change every day, every week, and every month. Each one is unique. Some are very independent and get along without much human help. Others are dependent upon special diets and require extra care and protection.

Something To Talk About

Like pets and like people, plants have names. Many have special nicknames that are different in different parts of the country, but they all have real names, given in Latin so that anyone, anywhere, can be sure that he is talking about a specific plant.

First is the genus name, like a person's surname. It indicates the closely related group that the plant belongs to. Then comes the species name, like a person's first name. Sometimes there is a third name to indicate a special variety. For example, a person's name may be Brown. His given name may be Robert, and people might say "He's the redheaded one" to distinguish him from his brothers. Try learning some of the botanical names of plants for indoor gardening. Try rolling them on the tongue. They are fun to say. Look for them on plant labels and in plant catalogs. Don't be afraid of them.

Some plants are such new imports that they do not have any nicknames as yet, and so are called by their botanical names, such as dieffenbachia. Some have botanical names that are very familiar, such as the begonia. Some have been grown for so long by so many people that they have many different nicknames in various parts of the country. Impatiens is one of these. It may be called Sultana, Busy Lizzie, Patience, or Periwinkle.

Learning about Plant Cells

Look at a piece of polished wood under a magnifying glass. That wood was once part of a tree (which is a plant), and those small cavities, each surrounded by a thick wall, were once living plant cells. Before that woody wall was formed, each one of those cells was like a tiny, living closed box, holding a quantity of fluid like watery gelatin. In the center was a large space called the vacuole, containing a liquid called cell sap. This thick fluid was the living matter, called protoplasm, similar to the protoplasm that human beings are made of.

All the activities of plants come from that semi-fluid protoplasm. It provides for growth, the passage of fluids up and down the plant's stem, the taking in of substances by the roots, the opening of buds, and the colors and arrangement of the flowers.

Learning about Seeds

Talk about the fact that the life of a plant starts with a seed. In each seed is an embryo plant, just waiting for moisture and warmth to start it growing into a plant like the one from which it came. Seeds carry their own food supply, enough to feed the young plant until it can make its own food from air, soil, and water. Seeds are little living miracles.

Learning about Roots

When the seed gets enough warmth and moisture the little root pushes its way out and bends downward into the soil. It is made up of cells, like all living things.

The cells at the root tip divide into two, and each of these divides, so that many new cells are formed and the root elongates. The cells inside the root expand, too, so that the root gets wider as well as longer.

For a time, the root feeds on the food supply stored in the seed. When this is gone it has to depend on food made by the plant leaves. It develops tiny root hairs that absorb water and dissolved minerals from the soil. These little root hairs are very fragile. Never pull a seedling out of the soil by its stem. It will break these root hairs. Lift a seedling out carefully with a knife blade or other implement. Shake off the soil and look for the root hairs. Then poke a hole in the soil, set the seedling carefully in it, and firm the soil around it so that the seedling can continue to grow.

These tiny root hairs live only a short time. They are always being replaced by new ones. The point of the root is always being replenished, too, somewhat like a piledriver in action. The older roots become woody and form an anchor for the plant. They act as a channel for getting and carrying liquid food into the stem. Water containing liquid food is conducted through the roots into the stem and leaves.

Plants get some of the raw materials for making food from the air, but they depend upon the roots to provide water and minerals. Roots are alive and need oxygen. The soil must be porous. Air must get to the roots so that they can breathe. The roots need moisture because they cannot absorb the mineral matter from the soil unless it is dissolved.

Talk about soil. The right kind of soil is very important. Soil is complex. It is made from the erosion of rocks by frost, thaw, rain, and wind. It consists of mineral particles plus organic material called humus. This humus is made from decayed plant and animal life and is very important because it not only lightens the soil, but also provides extra nutrients. Take a walk in the woods. Dig down through the layer of leaves until the soil is dark and porous. That layer is humus and is full of valuable plant food.

The size of the particles in the soil is important. If they are too big, water runs down through them and cannot get back up again. If they are too small, the soil gets caked and water runs off instead of into it.

A good soil provides the roots with nitrogen that encourages leaf growth, and with phosphorus and potassium for flowering and fruiting, as well as many other minerals and chemical food. Plants have the ability to change these soil nutrients into starches, sugars, and proteins.

Learning about the Shoot or Stem

Soon after the root has grown from the seed, a little shoot or stem appears and grows upwards toward the light and air. What it looks like is dependent upon what kind of plant it is. The first two leaves are usually smooth and often will not look at all like the plant's regular leaves. When the second or third pair of leaves form, the plant is ready for transplanting into its own little pot.

Watch the stem grow. It keeps elongating like the roots. The space between the nodes gets longer. *Nodes* are the places along the stem where leaves develop. Look in the axil of the leaf. Sometimes there is a bud that will turn into a branch of the plant.

Stems are not always above the soil. When they are below soil level they have various names. A *tuber,* for example, is an underground stem swollen with food storage. Look at a potato. It is really a swollen, underground stem. Notice the presence of buds, called "eyes", from which shoots grow. They prove that the tuber is really a stem.

A bulb is the thickened, lower part of a stem, surrounded by thick, fleshy leaves full of stored food. In the center of those leaves there is often a flower bud. Cut a tulip bulb in half vertically and see the whole new plant in miniature—leaves and flower.

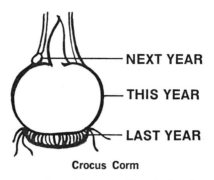

Crocus Corm

A corm is somewhat like a bulb. It is also the thickened part of a stem beneath the soil, but it does not have the fleshy leaves. When a corm grows flowers, it is exhausted and another corm forms on top of it for the next year's flower. Lift up a crocus corm after flowering and maturing. Note the new corm on top of the old. The new one will lift off easily.

Learning about Leaves

Look at a leaf carefully. It is the food factory of the plant. All the world's food supply is made by the leaves of green plants. Without plants, human life could not survive on earth. Talk about the life cycles of plants and animals.

The average leaf is a thin, flattened structure with an upper and a lower side. These sides are paved with cells. Through them run a network of vessels called *veins,* continuous with those of the stem and roots. On the lower side of the leaf are numerous openings or pores, called *stomata.* They are invisible to the naked eye.

The roots of the plant take in water that is carried through the veins into the leaves. There it meets carbon dioxide gas that is taken into the leaves from the air through the stomata. Using energy from the sun or artificial sources, the green leaves combine them into sugar. The food-making process in which light is used as a source of energy is called *photosynthesis.* It makes carbohydrates, which are sugars and starches. Some of these are turned into fats and proteins. Man has not yet learned to make food the way a green plant can!

The green substance in the leaves is called *chlorophyll*. It acts as a catalyst or agent in making food from water and carbon dioxide, using the sun's energy. That is why green plants must have light, air, and space for the leaves to get the light.

Look at the surface of a leaf. It has a waxy, transparent coating that lets the sunlight reach the food-making cells, and protects the leaf as well.

Study the veins of a leaf. They are the traffic routes for liquids in the plant. Water and dissolved minerals travel into the leaves. Food as dissolved sugar travels out through the stems. Veins also serve to stiffen the leaves and help to hold their shapes.

Touch the stem of a leaf. It lets the leaf flutter and move in the wind without breaking off.

Look at the edges of a leaf. Some are smooth, some are rough, some deeply indented. No two leaves are exactly alike.

Touch the surface of a leaf. Some are smooth and crisp. Others may be rubbery, or fuzzy, or soft as velvet. Compare the top surface of a leaf with its back. Do they look or feel alike? Look at the color of a leaf. Some have parts without chlorophyll. These have a substance called carotene in patches. It makes the colored foliage of plants like coleus.

Watch a plant that has been in the sun or wind too long. Notice how its leaves begin to hang down or wilt. That is because more moisture has evaporated from them than comes in through the roots, stem, and veins. This water loss is called *transpiration*. It never happens at night because there is no sun to evaporate the water. Often a plant will perk up and its leaves get fresh and crisp again in the night. Observe the effects of transpiration in outdoor plants after a very hot day, and then observe the same plants after a cool night.

Learning about Buds

Buds appear at the tips of the stems and in the axils of the leaves. Look for them. The former often become flowers; the latter usually become new branches of the plant.

Learning about Flowers

Look at a flower. It is at the end of a stem. Notice how the stem has thickened to form what looks like a little platform or case in which the flower parts are set.

Observe the lowest of the whorls or rings. It is made up of *sepals*. All the sepals together form the *calyx*. They are usually green and look like small leaves, but they can be colored. Some flowers have no calyx.

Look at the next whorl. These are called *petals,* and together they form the *corolla* of a flower. They are usually colored. They may be separate or joined together into a tube or trumpet shape. Sometimes the sepals and petals are so much alike that they are called the *perianth*.

Look inside the corolla and find one or more whorls of *stamens*. Note that each stamen is usually made up of two parts—a thin stem called the *filament;* and at the top, a thickened part called the *anther*. The pollen is produced in the anther. It is the male part of the flower. Open the anther carefully with a pin and see the pollen inside.

In the center of the flower there is a pistil, or sometimes several pistils. The pistil is the female part of the flower. It is usually made up of a swollen part called the *ovary,* containing one or more eggs, or *ovules*. The top of the pistil is often drawn into a neck, called the *style,* whose free end, the *stigma,* produces a sticky, sugary substance. The grains of pollen will stick to this, and so fertilize the ovules in the ovary. Touch the stigma. Feel how sticky it is. Pollen can fall on it and stick, or be brushed onto it by a bee or other insect attracted to the sugary substance, thus fertilizing the flower so that it can make seeds. The flower is the next-to-last step in a plant's life.

Learning about Plant Cycles

Making or "setting" seeds is the last step in a plant's life. It varies as to time. Some plants are *annuals*. Their seeds germinate in the spring, the plant comes up, blooms, and sets seeds in the same year. Then the plant dies. *Biennials* grow into plants the

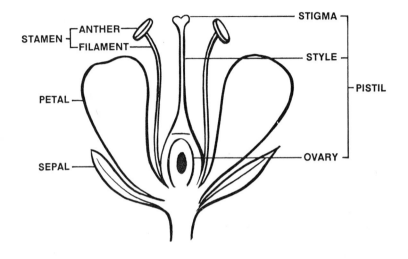

Parts of a Flower

first year but do not bloom. The leaves make large amounts of food that is stored over the winter. In the next spring the leaves are followed by flowers and seeds, and then the plant dies. The carrot is a biennial. That big root is a storage of food for its own use the next year.

A *perennial* plant may live a few years without flowering, although sometimes a perennial will bloom the first year. After it blooms the first time, it will bloom again every year for many years. Many plants used in indoor gardening are perennials.

Plants must flower to make seeds. Seeds are the fusion of the male and female cells of the pollen grains and the ovules.

Something To Do

How do plants get water? Prove that it rises from the soil up through the roots, then into the stems and leaves. Put the bottom of a stalk of celery into a glass of water that has been colored red or blue with food coloring. Let it stand overnight. Then cut the stalk above the waterline and look for the red or blue coloring. Or put a white carnation into water colored green. The next day—a green carnation!

Watch root hairs. Plant a few beans in wet sand, peat moss, or other starting mixture. When they germinate, take one out very carefully, using toothpicks to lift it gently. Shake off the starting mixture and look at the tiny root hairs. In a day or so take out another sprouting bean and note the difference in its root hairs. They will not be identical with the other.

Test for starch. Boil a peeled potato in a small amount of water. Take it out and add a few drops of iodine to the water. If starch is there the solution will turn blue-black.

Can leaves form starch? Test one and see. Select a leaf on a growing plant. Cover part of that leaf with foil to remove all light. Put the leaf in bright light for at least a day. Then remove the leaf from the plant and dip it into boiling water to kill it. Rub it with warm alcohol to remove the green coloring. Pour a few drops of iodine onto the leaf. The part of the leaf that has been soaking in the sun will give the starch reaction, but the part that was covered by the foil will not.

Find out what a bud looks like inside. A Brussels sprout is a large bud. Cut one vertically in half. Notice the nodes, leaves, buds, and internodes. Cut open a rosebud or other flower bud. Notice the sepals, petals, stamens, carpel, and ovules.

Do plants need and want the light? Set a plant on a window sill or table near a window. Do not move it. In a week notice how the plant has leaned toward the light. Turn it around and leave it for another week. What happens?

CHAPTER 2

How to Grow Plants

Plants grow from seeds, but do not always "come true" and produce plants exactly like the parent plant. This quality of possible variation makes it very interesting to grow plants from seeds. The slight variations that may be produced are fun to discover.

For true-to-parent plants, *cuttings* from the parent plant can be rooted. Plants formed by *layering* also will be identical and so will plants formed by *air layering,* a process of propagation first used by the Chinese.

Something To Talk About

Before trying any of these ways to propagate plants, talk about what will be needed in the way of containers, tools, and supplies. Look around. Use what is at hand when possible. Assemble throw-away containers for starting seeds and cuttings. Wax or plastic milk containers with one long side cut out and the open end closed with masking tape or a paper clip make very satisfactory "flats" for planting seeds. When cut in half through the middle, they make good pots for cuttings. The round cardboard or plastic containers for salads and cottage cheese are also useful. So are old muffin tins. Coffee cans are fine, and can be painted green or white for permanent use as pots. Pretzel and potato chip cans are good for large plants. Of course the usual clay or plastic pots are always fine. They can be bought at the garden center, plant nursery, or florist shop.

Foil pans of various sizes are very good to put under pots to keep water from staining the furniture.

Any container used for a pot for seeds or cuttings should have drainage holes in the bottom. Bits of broken clay pots, called "crocks", should be placed over the drainage holes, or a layer of pebbles should cover the bottom to keep the soil from coming out of the pot, but allowing the water to drain off.

In addition to containers, talk about simple tools to make the work easier. An old pair of scissors will be useful. So will an old kitchen spoon and fork. A knife, some small stakes or tongue depressors for labeling seed rows, a spray bottle for watering seedlings, and a watering can for plants will be needed.

Something To Do

For supplies, visit a garden center or the garden counters of a supermarket. Buy a bag of peat or sphagnum moss, a bag of potting soil, and some vermiculite or perlite, some sharp sand, like that used in the bottoms of bird cages and aquariums. A bottle of liquid fertilizer will be needed later.

Learning about Seeding

Put crocks or pebbles over the drainage holes of a container. Then add a layer of moist peat or sphagnum moss to conserve moisture. Mix the potting soil with some of the moss and the coarse sand. Fill the container to within a half-inch of the top, then water it thoroughly. Press the seeds lightly into the soil and cover with soil to twice the thickness of the seed. Spray gently with water so that the top is moist. Then place the container in semi-shade, where the temperature is from sixty-five to seventy-five degrees. If the air in the room is dry, cover the container with glass or plastic. Remove it and wipe off any moisture that forms. Remove it, too, when the seeds sprout.

Seeds can be sown in moist peat or sphagnum moss, or in moist sand alone, but they will have to be transplanted very promptly. These mixtures will not provide any food for the small plants.

When the seedlings come up, move them into gradual sun and keep them moist but not soggy. Use the spray bottle so that you don't knock them over. Once a week feed the little plants. Use a liquid fertilizer such as Hyponex, Rapid-Gro, Plant Marvel, or other trade name. Use only at half strength. Transplant the seedlings when they have grown their second or third set of leaves.

Try raising coleus, Jerusalem cherry, Christmas peppers, and geraniums from seed. They all germinate easily and make delightful little plants to keep or to give away.

Learning about Transplanting

The roots will develop many delicate little root hairs. Lift the seedlings out with soil still on the roots. Set each into a hole dug in the soil of a new pot. Cover it to the stem level and firm the soil gently around it. A pencil makes a good tamper. Then water the plant gently to settle the soil around the roots. Keep the plant out of drafts and out of the direct sun until it gets over the shock of transplanting.

Re-pot a plant when the roots start coming out of the drainage holes. Small plants do not like big pots. Always use the next size pot when transplanting. Size is measured by the diameter across the top.

To get a plant out of its pot and ready for a larger one, first water it thoroughly. Then invert the pot over the left hand, holding the stem of the plant between the first and second fingers. Tap the bottom of the pot with a knife or other object. The entire soil ball will be released. Make sure that the new pot has a crock in the bottom and a layer of peat or sphagnum moss. Then set the plant and its soil in the new pot, fill the sides in with fresh soil, firm it all around the plant, and give the new pot a good watering.

Learning about Cuttings

A cutting is a piece of the plant that can be made to root and grow and become a plant exactly like its parent. There are three major types of cuttings: stem cuttings, leaf cuttings, and root cuttings. The first two are most often used in indoor gardening.

Stem cuttings sometimes happen accidentally. Watch pussy willows or forsythia in a vase of water. After several weeks look at the underwater stems. Chances are that many of them have developed roots. These can be planted in soil when the roots are about an inch long. Presto! A new shrub!

To root the stem of a houseplant in water, cut a piece from two to six inches long, with several nodes or joints on it. Make the cut a third of an inch below a node. To keep it making food leave the foliage on it, except for under the water line. Let the end of the cutting dry out for an hour or so before putting it in water, but keep the leaves moist to prevent wilting. Then put the cutting into a glass or bottle of water. Roots prefer darkness, so put a piece of paper or foil around the container to keep out the light. Transplant the cutting into a pot with soil when the roots are about a half-inch long.

The same process can be used with soil. For best results, let the cutting dry but keep the leaves moist as above. Then dust the cut with a plant hormone from the garden center or florist. Such a powder is a chemical product that produces growth activity in the cutting, thus encouraging rooting and growth. After dusting the cut, insert it two or three joints deep into any sterile rooting mixture such as sphagnum or peat moss, sand, vermiculite, or potting soil. Cover the cutting with a glass, or a plastic bag held in place by stakes. Put the pot in a warm room but not in direct sunlight. Transplant it into potting soil, if other mixture has been used, after roots have formed.

Begonias, geraniums, coleus, lantana, philodendron, ivy,

34

Coleus Cutting

poinsettia, and shrimp plants are only a few of the many house-plants that grow easily from stem cuttings.

Leaf cuttings are an easy way to start new plants. Use fleshy, healthy leaves, not old ones. Take them from the middle of the plant, not from the outside.

One way is to root the stem of the leaf in water. African violets are often propagated this way. Cut the leaf off with a stem about two inches long if possible. Fill a glass with water and cut a piece of cardboard to fit over the top of the glass. Cut a hole in the cardboard large enough for the stem to fit through it, so that the stem is in the water while the leaf is held up by the cardboard. Then insert the stem. It will root in the water. When roots are plain to see, carefully cut away the cardboard and put the rooted stem into a pot of soil made of a mixture of humus, potting soil, and sand.

Another method is to stick the whole length of the leaf stem into a moist soil mixture so that the bottom of the leaf touches the soil. Keep moist. Cover with a glass or a plastic bag. Eventually small plants will start at the base of the leaf.

Try rooting a Rex begonia leaf. Remove the leaf with a small piece of stem. Place it flat on moist sand, stem stuck into it. Make cuts across the main veins of the leaf. Peg the leaf down. Little plants will grow at the cut veins.

Snake plants propagate easily. Cut a leaf into pieces from three to six inches long. Place them upright in a moist rooting mixture.

One of the queerest leaves to watch is from the Kalanchoe. Young plants will grow at the tips and around the edges of a cut leaf even if it is not planted. Pin a leaf to a curtain and watch. For permanent rooting, pin a leaf down flat on a moist rooting mixture.

Learning about Layering

Layering is a simple process that often happens all by itself in the outdoor garden. A trailing rosebush, a dangling branch of a forsythia bush, or a long stem of ivy will be in contact with the ground, perhaps held down by dead leaves. At the point of contact, roots often form, and a new plant thus grows by the side of its parent plant.

Indoors, many such vines as ivy can be encouraged to layer. Fill a pot with potting soil and place it by the side of the pot holding the vine. Sometimes it helps if the second pot is a bit lower than the pot in which the vine is growing. Bend a long stem of the vine over, and place it so that it lies across the soil in the second pot. At the center of this stem, on the underside, nick it slightly, and bury the nicked area in the soil. If necessary, hold the stem down with pebbles or a clothespin, to make sure of good contact with the soil. Roots will form at the nick. Dusting the nick with a hormone powder will facilitate rooting. When this happens, cut off the part of the stem nearer the parent plant. The end, or tip, with its new roots, becomes a new plant, exactly like its parent.

Air layering is a fascinating process. It is a way to produce a smaller plant from the top of a large one by getting roots to form high up on the stem. Then the top can be cut off and potted to form a new plant. At the same time, an overly-large plant has been cut down in size.

To air layer, make a shallow cut three-quarters of the way around the stem and about a half-inch wide. Go through the outer bark but *not* the center, woody part. Dust the cut with a rooting hormone powder, available from garden centers and florist shops.

Then wrap the cut in moist sphagnum moss an inch and a half thick. Cover this moss mass with plastic film and fasten it at the top and bottom with string or a twistem so that the moss will not dry out or move down. Open the film occasionally to make sure that the moss is still damp. Wet it again if necessary, then re-tie the film. Keep the plant in a warm, moist, shady place. The moss will get full of roots in seven to ten weeks.

When this happens, cut the stem of the plant just below the roots and put the roots, moss, and all, into a pot with soil. Water it well, and keep the humidity high. The pot should not be more than two inches wider than the rooted section. Too large a pot will retard growth.

If the plant is very thin-stemmed and it would be hard to make a circular cut, make a notch cut. Be careful not to cut through the stem. Make the cut *upward* into the stem a few inches below the crown. The cut should be about an inch or so long, and should go from a quarter to a third of an inch into the stem. Keep the cut open by inserting a toothpick, small pebble, or other object. Dust it with the rooting powder, cover it with the moss as above. Stake the plant if it seems top-heavy.

After the new plant has been potted keep the bottom of the old plant, even though it has been beheaded. Usually it will send out new shoots from the bottom and will get bushy.

For more plants, cut off parts of the stem that were left below the cut-off part. Cut these into sections so that each will have some nodes, or "eyes." Lay these sideways in a moist sand and peat moss mixture. Eventually leaves will push up and roots develop. Cut the little plants apart and put each into a pot. New plants from old!

Many of the large foliage plants can be air layered. Try it when the plant gets leggy or grows too tall. Dieffenbachia, schefflera (umbrella plant), rubber plant, and dracaena (dragon plant) are good plants for air layering.

Learning about General Care of Plants

Give plants tender loving care, and they will respond by thriving for you. Here are a few tips:

Use tepid water when watering. Let the water sit overnight to eliminate chlorine or other chemicals. Water well. Do not just sprinkle. BUT—do not overwater. Plants should not sit in water; their roots need air. Water from the bottom sometimes. Sink the pot in water up to several inches. Take it out of the water when the top becomes moist. Then let it sit until excess water is drained off.

Group plants together. Most of them seem to like company, and the grouping helps to raise the humidity. Put the pot of a plant that needs high humidity into a larger pot or jardiniere, and stuff the spaces between with moist sphagnum moss. Dig and loosen the soil in the top of the pot. Fertilize the plant regularly but lightly. Cigar or cigarette ashes are good for plants. They contain potassium.

When re-potting, always use fresh, unused soil. Re-pot about every two years or whenever the roots of the plant start to come out of the bottom of the pot.

If the leaves of a plant get brown at the tips, cut down on water or fertilizer. If the leaves get brown and curl, the air may be too warm or dry. When leaves drop off, check for drafts, for over-feeding, or for too dry a room.

Learning about Vacation Care of Plants

If the vacation will not last too long, most plants, including foliage plants, can survive if given a bit of forethought. Probably the best answer is to have a friend or neighbor come in every few days and water them.

This is not always possible. There is another method for all but the tallest and bushiest plants. Water the plants well. Then cover each plant with a plastic bag large enough to cover pot and all, and kept from touching the leaves by sticks or stakes set into the pot. Tie the bag at the top with a rubber band or a twistem. Use a large garment bag for a tall plant. Plants so treated can exist without care for several weeks.

If the vacation is for a long time, farm the plants out to friends or neighbors, board them at a local plant nursery or florist shop, or hire a reliable person to come in once or twice a week to care for them. Don't abandon the plants—they are part of the family!

CHAPTER 3

About Plant Diseases and Pests

Something To Talk About

Precaution, as with human diseases and disorders, is far easier to practice than is curing. Plants are like members of the family. The best way to keep them healthy and happy is to make sure that they are clean and in clean surroundings, well-fed, protected, and loved. Encourage the child to look at them every day, not only to admire their beauty and to watch their growth, but also to be on the lookout for any signs of disease or plant pests. A curled up leaf, a flabby stem, a brown tip, a wilted look—all may be signs of trouble.

Learning What Plants Need

Like people, plants need fresh air, clean water, and food that agrees with them. They need protection from too much sun and heat, too much cold, drafts, and air that is too dry. If they are given loving, daily attention, they will get all these environmental needs.

Some very successful Green Thumbers believe that plants respond and flourish when they are talked to. Actually, the human breath with its carbon dioxide, which plants need, may be helpful, so perhaps talking or singing to plants really may help them to grow. Try it and see how it works.

Some people believe that plants respond to melodic, happy-sounding music. At least one experiment by a scientist with a machine somewhat like a lie-detector seems to indicate that plants respond physically to music and flattery, or to threats and verbal abuse. He attaches this machine to a leaf and records the response through an electric impulse like that registered by an electrocardiograph machine. He claims that plants respond with violent reaction when they are frightened or unhappy, and relax when they are reassured and praised.

Plants have many things in common with humans. Experiment. Try telling them how handsome they are and how well they are growing. It may have a very important result. By really looking at them, admiring and praising them, any disease or pest is much more likely to be seen, caught, and corrected. Encourage the child to spend some time daily in inspecting the plants.

Learning to Avoid Plant Diseases

Try to prevent plant diseases, because they are hard to cure in a home setting where spraying and isolation can be problems. Make sure that the flowerpots and windowboxes are kept clean. Wipe off any deposits of salts along the edges. Do not let the bottoms get slimy or the sides get moldy.

Be very careful when buying a plant. Look it over very carefully. Do not buy it if the leaves look scaly or unhealthy. Be careful, too, in bringing home any cuttings or leaves from school or from other places. Keep a new plant, slip, or cutting away from the other plants for several days to make sure that it is healthy and has nothing contagious.

In buying seeds or plants, always ask for disease-resistant types. If a plant does get a disease, isolate it at once. If it does not respond to treatment, get rid of it. Burn the infected parts. The spores of many plant diseases can spread very easily and quickly.

Do not feed a sick plant or a plant that has just been re-potted or transplanted. Would you feed a steak dinner to a patient just recovering from a major operation? Do not fertilize a plant until you make sure that the soil of the pot is moist. Otherwise the fertilizer may burn the stems and root.

Children enjoy washing and spraying the leaves to keep them healthy and clean, or dusting curly, fuzzy, or plushy leaves with a soft brush.

Damping off is the most dread disease of seedlings. It is caused by a fungus that spreads quickly and destroys the stems of the young plants. Prevent it by using only sterile soil, vermiculite, or peat moss when starting the seeds. Always read the labels when buying bags of planting soil. Make sure they have been sterilized.

Before planting seeds, cover them with a fungicide preventative that can be bought at garden centers or wherever seeds are sold. It goes by various names, such as Arosan and Samesan. Tear off a corner of the seed packet. Drop in just enough of the powder to cover the tip of the little finger. Fold the corner of the seed packet and shake well, so that every seed will get a light dusting. Then plant the seeds in a sterile starting mixture or soil in clean pots or other containers. If the pots are new and made of clay, soak them overnight in water. Otherwise they may absorb too much moisture from the soil.

Mold or mildew on leaves or stems is due to over-crowding, not enough ventilation, and not enough light. Molds and mildews spread. Isolate the affected plant and dust it with sulphur. Dusting sulphur can be bought at most garden centers, plant nurseries, and florist shops.

Learning about Indoor Plant Pests

The chief pests in the indoor garden are insects. An insect has three pairs of legs. It has three body parts, a head, a thorax, and an abdomen covered with a protective shield. It breathes by *spiracles* or pores along its body. Its mouth is adapted for chewing or sucking. Look at one through a magnifying glass.

Red spider mites are so small that they are invisible to the naked eye. Feel the underside of a plant leaf. If it feels rough and webby the trouble may be caused by the red spider mite. Prevention is easier than the cure. Spray the leaves weekly and the mites will be washed away. The mites are very fond of certain plants like ivy. Inspect these carefully every day.

Aphids are often called plant lice. They have tiny, soft bodies, and various types are various colors: some white, some green, pink, red, yellow, or brown. They are sucking insects. They cluster on new shoots or in buds or inside curled-up leaves. They are so small and so protectively colored that they are hard to see.

A rotenone-pyrethrum aerosol bomb spray is the best way to kill aphids on indoor plants. These aerosol sprays are sold in most garden shops, supermarkets, and other places selling seeds and plants. Read the directions carefully. Do not over-spray.

Mealybugs are small, sucking insects, also. They are usually found in the leaf axils of houseplants. Their bodies are flat and a powdery, waxy white in color.

Dip a cotton swab or a toothpick with a bit of cotton on its tip, into alcohol and gently remove the mealybugs. Watch the plant carefully for a re-infestation, and the mealybugs can be controlled.

Cyclamen mites are very tiny, almost invisible insects that can infest cyclamen and African violets. They cause deformed center leaves and distorted stems. When they occur the best thing to do is to destroy the plant. Their control is too difficult for the average houseplant owner.

Safety Rules For Using Pesticides

Pesticides, whether in solutions or in dust form, all contain substances that are harmful to people and pets. Use them with great care and discretion, only when needed, and in small doses. Remember the following rules and teach them to the child:

Read directions carefully. Do not increase the dosage. Do not over-spray or over-dust. Several light sprayings or dustings are much more helpful than one overly heavy one.

Cover any fishbowl, aquarium, pet dish, bird cage, and other such equipment. Never spray near food or food containers.

Do not smoke while spraying or dusting. The material may be inflammable. Also, you are more likely to inhale the spray or dust.

Always wash hands and arms thoroughly and *at once* when the spraying or dusting is over. The skin may be sensitive to the ingredients.

Keep out of the drift of the spray or dust. Try not to breathe any of it into the lungs.

Keep the can, bottle, or aerosol bomb out of the reach of children and pets.

Never store the can, bottle, or aerosol bomb in a food cabinet.

Get rid of the empty container *at once*. Wash a glass or metal can or bottle before throwing it into the garbage. Never put an aerosol bomb can into an incinerator or fire.

Part II

INDOOR GARDENING GALORE

CHAPTER 4

Gardening Fun with Kitchen Throw-aways

The kitchen is full of child-easy gardening projects. Its atmosphere is friendly and relaxed. It's just the place to talk about food and where it comes from, what it looks like, how it grows.

Something To Talk About

Learning about Vegetables and Fruits

Visit the grocery store or supermarket together. Browse along the bins filled with vegetables and fruits. Name them all. Notice their many shapes, colors, textures of the outside, their sizes, their smells.

Talk about where they came from and how far back in history many of them go. (See PART IV of *Learning About Nature Through Crafts.*) The so-called Irish potato really comes from South America. Spanish explorers found South American Indians cultivating potatoes in the sixteenth century. They brought potatoes to Europe. It became the biggest crop grown in Ireland, and got its present name from there.

Onions, turnips, and radishes are the three most ancient vegetables. They have been grown for food for over four thousand years. Talk about the possible reasons for this, such as their being very hardy, easily stored, plus giving flavor to meat dishes.

Peas come from Europe, where they grew wild. Carrots grew wild in the temperate parts of Asia and have been harvested for food for over two thousand years.

Beets originally came from the Canary Islands. The Greeks named them after the letter "B" because they thought the seeds looked like that letter. Look at a beet seed and see if it does.

Lemons and oranges first grew from Southeast Asia to the Mediterranean Sea. The Arabs introduced them into Europe. Grapefruit came originally from the West Indies. Now all these fruits are grown in Florida, Texas, and California.

Talk about what parts of plants we eat. Endive, lettuce, cabbage, parsley, and kale are *leaves* from plants. Cauliflower, broccoli, and Brussels sprouts are *buds*. Beets, turnips, carrots, and radishes are *roots*. Apples, oranges, tomatoes, and melons are *fruits*. Inside them are *seeds*. Look at them and see how different all these seeds are.

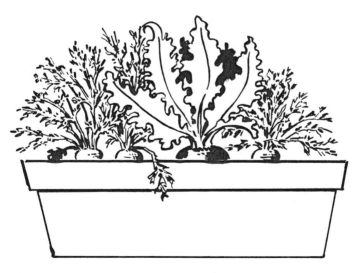

Carrots and Beet

Turnip Top

Something To Do

Learning To Use Kitchen Throw-aways

They are natural interest-starters in indoor gardening. With little effort and expense, the child and adult can work together in growing some fruits and vegetables, using their seeds and roots to find out what the plants are like. Try some of the following experiments and discuss them as the projects progress, or while waiting for results.

Apples. Select a ripe apple and quarter it. Notice how the seeds are arranged. Pick some of them out. Wash them off, dry them, and plant them in potting soil in a milk container cut lengthwise. Cover them with about a quarter of an inch of soil, moisten the top, and be patient. Some of the seeds should germinate. When leaves appear, bring out into the light gradually.

Avocado. Note how large the seed is, how easy to prepare for growing. Select a fully ripe avocado, as soft as possible. Those from Florida have dark green, rough skin and their pulp is softer and oilier. California avocados are more oval and thinner skinned. The seed from the Florida ones germinates more easily and grows faster.

Halve it carefully, so as not to cut into the seed. If the seed has already sprouted, rinse it off carefully and plant it in potting soil. Leave the tip of the seed outside. Avocado seeds like light.

If the seed has not sprouted, rinse it and put it in a warm place overnight, so that the dark, outer skin will come off easily. Then plant it in a fairly large pot, around seven inches in diameter. The soil should be two-thirds potting soil, one-third humus, plus some sand or vermiculite to make it porous.

Plant the larger, flatter end down, leaving one-third of the pit exposed. Water the soil well, and put a glass or plastic bag over the pot to keep it moist. The pit will split open in about a month. When the little stem gets about four inches high, add an inch and a half of soil to the pot to cover the seed.

Notice the growing habit of the plant. It will grow straight up for several feet before it will branch. It can be pruned by cutting two inches off the top, diagonally, when the little plant is about six inches tall. It will then grow a new shoot near the base and will be bushier. Do not prune it if you want a tall, tree-like plant.

Transplant it as it grows taller. A rule of thumb is that plants should not be taller than six times the diameter of the pot.

Indoor avocados seldom flower or bear fruit, but they make beautiful houseplants. They need sun. Turn the pot twice a week to keep the plant growing straight, or keep it in a place where it gets full sun.

Try rooting a seed in water. Use toothpicks to suspend the seed at the top of a glass of water so that the thick end just touches the water. Keep it in a dark place for six or seven weeks, or until a large taproot emerges. Then move it into the light.

Avocado

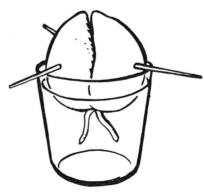

Avocado Seed Rooting in Water

The green stem will start to grow and the plant can then be potted in soil. Try growing avocado seeds by both methods, soil and water, and compare the final results.

Beans. Watch how a bean sprouts. Soak several lima beans overnight in water. Then fill a jelly or water glass with moist soil or sand, and plant the beans about a half inch deep, up against the sides of the glass so that they will be visible from the outside. Cover the outside of the glass with foil or paper for the first few days to provide darkness for the beans to sprout. Then look at them. The little root will have formed, pushing down into the soil. Before long, the little stem will push up towards the light, and leaves will emerge.

Find out how strong seeds are, and how much force they can exert. Fill a small jar with dried beans or peas. Add water. Cover the top of the jar with a thin, flat piece of wood or heavy

Dried Beans

cardboard. Put a small rock on top. Look at the jar daily. As the beans or peas begin to swell in germination they will lift that stone.

Carrots are a storehouse of food for new plants. Try some carrot projects. Cut an inch or so off the top of a carrot. Plant this top in moist sand, vermiculite, or other rooting mixture, keeping the top of the carrot out of the mixture. Moisten and keep in a dark place. In about a week look for new green leaves starting to develop.

Grow them in water. Get a big, old carrot. Cut off the top and three-fourths of the bottom. Fill a small glass with water. Put toothpicks into the carrot on three sides near the top, so that they hold the carrot halfway out of the water. Keep the water level up. After a while, fern-like carrot leaves will start to grow.

Try growing a carrot upside down. Cut off the bottom of a long carrot about a third of the way up. Scoop out carefully a good part of the bottom of the carrot. Poke a hole on each side of the scooped out part and run a piece of string through the holes. Hang the carrot up, upside down. Fill the scooped out place with water and keep it filled. Carrot leaves will start to grow out of the bottom and curve upward. Try these experiments with beets or turnips.

Citrus Fruits. Grow orange, grapefruit, lemon, and tangerine seeds. They make very pretty indoor plants. Pick out nice, plump seeds from well-developed, ripe fruit, or they will not germinate. Rinse the seeds off and soak them in water for twenty-four hours. Then plant them in a milk carton "flat" that has holes punched out of the bottom for drainage. Label the different rows or containers, because the little plants will all look very much alike. A mixture of potting soil and peat moss makes a good starting soil. Add a bit of sand or vermiculite to make it porous. Plant the seeds about an inch apart. Cover the seeds with about a half inch of moist soil. The soil must never dry out. Cover the top of the container with a paper towel and keep in a warm place. The seeds may germinate in about ten days. When the first leaves come up, put the plants in the light, and in another few days into sunlight. When the seedlings are about ten days old, cut off the ones that are too crowded. When the remainder have made their second or third pair of leaves, transplant them

Grapefruit

carefully into separate pots. As the plants grow, admire their shiny, bright leaves. Re-pot the plants when necessary.

Dates are interesting. Their seeds grow into dainty palm trees. Most dates in stores and in packages have been treated, however, and will not germinate. Try to find some untreated dates without sulphur at a health food store. Wash the date seed in tepid water and dry it. Plant it in a pot with potting soil mixed with peat moss and sand. Cover the seed with soil the thickness of the seed. Let the surface soil dry out between waterings. Put the container in a dark place and be very patient. The seed may take a long time, even months, to germinate. When it does, bring the plant into the light. It makes a lovely houseplant. It likes a cool temperature from fifty-five to sixty-five degrees, but it is quite tolerant in its needs.

Coffee beans in stores have been roasted and cannot germinate. Look at them, though, before they are ground. Notice their shape. Try to buy some coffee seeds from a seed company (see Resources). The seeds are red. Plant them in a mixture of potting soil, peat moss, and sand. Keep them moist and warm —and be very patient. They take a long time to germinate, but they make lovely, bushy little plants that will have small, very fragrant, white blossoms.

Mango seeds are flat and look a bit like large lima beans. In the tropics mangos grow to be ninety feet tall, but indoors they stay a reasonable height. They are evergreen, with dark, shiny leaves, natives of northeast India, Burma, and Thailand.

Buy the ripest fruit available. Remove the pulp. Scrape the seed with a knife and wash off all the flesh. The hairs will not come off. Let the pit soak in tepid water for a week, changing the water daily. Then plant the pit with its eye up, on edge, not flat, about an inch deep, and keep the soil moist. The soil should be the usual mixture of potting soil, peat moss, and sand. Do not try growing mango seeds unless you are patient. They may take as long as four months to germinate, or may take much less time. Plant several because they won't all germinate.

When the leaves push up they will be a dark red, then change to dark green and form a very pretty plant. When the mango is growing well, water it twice a week for three weeks and then

Pineapple Crown

let it dry out for a week. It likes a warm, moist room and is very sensitive to drafts. Keep it away from cold windows and open doors.

Pineapples are fascinating to grow. Buy one that has a well-shaped crown or top. When ready to plant, cut off this crown, leaving about an inch of the fruit on it. Let it sit for a day or two to dry out a bit. Then plant the fleshy bottom in the usual planting mixture. The pot can be fairly shallow, because pineapples have very shallow roots.

They belong to the Bromeliad family and are called "epiphytic" because they get food through their crowns, from the rain or dew. Note the "vase" that the leaves make around the stem. Keep this vase filled with water. Add a very weak solution of fertilizer after the plant has rooted. It should become well rooted in five to eight weeks. Watch it. It may develop a new shoot at the base of the crown.

The flowers form on a long stem rising high above the crown. These are called an "inflorescence," and fuse together to form the small pineapples. It takes the plant two years or more to mature and bear fruit, but the plant is an interesting one to observe.

Pineapple Plant

The pineapple plant likes temperatures of seventy-five to eighty-five degrees and several hours of light a day. Bright light will make the leaves turn a handsome, reddish shade.

It is said that a whole, ripe apple placed in the pot will make a pineapple set and bear fruit after flowering. The apple is said to release a chemical that helps the fruiting of the pineapple— the same chemical that gives the apple its distinctive aroma. Try this experiment with a flowering pineapple and see if it works.

Potatoes are fun to experiment with. Scoop out part of a large potato. Add matchsticks or golf tees for legs, and a bit of uncoiled rope for a tail. Fill the hole in the potato with an inch or so of soil, moisten it, and press in some grass seeds. Then watch the big potato get a green back. Keep the grass cut with scissors. Discard when the potato gets soft or discolored.

Sweet potatoes are often treated to prevent them from sprouting. Sometimes, though, a sweet potato in a store will show signs of sprouting. Buy that potato and place the tapered end in a jar or glass so that the tip touches water. It will make roots and send up leaves that grow into a very pretty vine if the potato is transplanted into a pot of soil.

54

CHAPTER 5

Raising Exotic Herbs for Cooking Use

The herbs grown indoors in a sunny window are *culinary* herbs, used in the preparation of food. The word "herb" comes from the Latin and means "grass".

Something To Talk About

Talk about the fact that herbs are centuries old; how most monasteries had extensive herb gardens; how the owners of castles grew the herbs used in their own kitchens. Discuss the reasons that herbs were so popular in early days; that there was no refrigeration, and so most meat would spoil and other foods become smelly; that herbs covered up these spoiled smells and made the food taste and smell much better.

Talk about the various herb families. Onions, chives, and shallots all belong to the big Lily family. Sweet marjoram, oregano, thyme, sweet basil, rosemary, and sage belong to the wide Mint family. Roll the stem of any of these between the fingers. Note that the stems are square not round—a sure sign

Sweet Basil

of the Mint family. The Parsley family is another large one, but most of its members, except for parsley, are not suitable for indoor gardening.

Culinary herbs, because of the odors of their leaves and stems, are called aromatic herbs. Dried, they are sold in jars and bottles and are part of the herb and spice shelf in the kitchen and in the supermarket. Take a look at them and see how the herbs look when dried. Are the leaves still whole? Have they been shredded or powdered? Experiment in using the dried herbs sometimes in food. Then try fresh herbs. Can you tell the difference?

Most culinary herbs are perennials. Among the best for indoor gardening are chives, sage, sweet marjoram, thyme, mint, rosemary, and tarragon. Basil, however, is an annual, and parsley a biennial.

Something To Do

Learning To Grow Herbs

Most herbs need sun. A glass shelf across a sunny kitchen window can hold pots or small containers of many herbs for

Herb Garden

family use. Some, like sage and basil, grow bushy and tall, but can be kept pruned into shape once they are well established.

Try growing most of them from seeds bought from the garden center or seed company. Potting soil with peat moss and a bit of sand makes a good mixture.

The seeds should be covered lightly with soil to the depth of the size of the seed. Most will germinate in about two weeks or less. Parsley takes considerably longer. Keep the soil moist but not soggy. When the leaves appear use a spray bottle to keep from flattening them. They will be mature enough to use in four to six weeks.

If a plant gets too large, snip off parts and freeze them for future use. Be careful in using fresh herbs. Taste the food as you use them. It takes more fresh herbs than dried herbs to give the right flavor.

Many plant nurseries and garden centers sell herbs in pots. Buy some if time is short or if you wish to get acquainted with them before growing them from seed. Either way, a row of sweet-smelling herbs makes a very cheerful sight and provides new experiences.

Learning about Special Herbs

Some herbs are tall, some very short. Some have green leaves, others have grayish ones. Some are very aromatic, others delicate in odor and taste. Learn to distinguish them by smell. Rub a leaf between the fingers. Nibble a leaf. Try raising some of the old-time favorites:

Basil germinates quite quickly and grows into a large plant unless kept pruned back by cutting and using the leaves. It likes light rather than strong sun. It will become branchy with fairly large leaves and grow to be eighteen inches tall. Cut off any flower stalks as they form, because the plant will die if allowed to go to seed. Basil's original home is Africa.

Dice up basil leaves and use them in soups, sauces, and egg dishes. It has a natural affinity with tomatoes. Use basil leaves with any dish of raw or cooked tomatoes.

Chives

Chives, like onions, belong to the big Lily family. Grow them from seed, or from "sets." These are small, immature onions that were produced by close planting the season before. They can be bought from a plant nursery or garden center. Seeds take longer; so sets are easier to grow. Give each set about five inches of room because it will spread. The plants will grow eight to ten inches tall. They will develop pretty little pin-cushiony lavender flowers. After flowering, cut the plant down and it will make new growth. In using chives, cut off one of the long, stem-like leaves near the base and chop it up in salads or any food where a delicate onion flavor will be good.

Marjoram comes in two types: sweet marjoram and wild marjoram, called oregano. They came originally from France and from Chile. Sweet marjoram has small, velvety, gray-green leaves and is very aromatic. Oregano has rather coarse, hairy, dark leaves. The flowers of both are pinkish white.

Their seeds are very small and take quite a while to germinate. When they come up they like sun. Pick leaves for use in seasoning when the plants are growing well. Use them in meat sauces, stews, and with sliced tomatoes and cucumbers. They are the best herbs for seasoning mushrooms.

Mint grown for seasoning is the spearmint variety. There is a variety that smells like oranges. Usually it is wise to buy a pot of mint. It grows from one to two feet tall, in shade or semi-shade, and it likes moisture. Use it in drinks and sauces.

Parsley seeds take several weeks to germinate; so many people prefer to buy a pot from the grocery store or garden center. As a biennial it makes its leaves the first year and develops the flowering stalk with small, yellowish green fruits the next year. One variety has dark green, flat leaves, but the usual variety has pretty green, curly leaves.

It likes full sun and is low-growing, getting only six to eight inches tall. In using it, always take off the outer leaves, leaving the inside ones to grow. Cut it up and use it fresh or dry it out and store for future use. It is excellent in salads and stews and as a garnish for meats and vegetables. Parsley originally grew wild in southern Europe.

Rosemary is also a native of southern Europe. Grow it from seed or buy it as a small plant. It likes good drainage, full sun, and soil that is not too rich. It will grow one to two feet tall and gets bushy. Its leaves are evergreen, long and narrow, and it develops clusters of small blue flowers. Propagate it by stem cuttings in water or moist sand. Rosemary is very aromatic. Use the leaves in any kind of lamb dish or with chicken, boiled potatoes, sauces, or biscuit dough.

Rosemary has a pretty legend. In Europe it grows very tall and bushy. Legend says that the Virgin Mary, in Her flight into Egypt, hung the clothes of the Infant Jesus on a rosemary bush to dry. Ever since, it has had bright blue flowers like the Virgin's robe, and has been called after the Holy Mother.

Sage can be started from seed. It will grow one to two feet tall but can be kept pruned back. Its leaves are gray with a woolly texture and a slightly pebbled surface. Use the leaves fresh or dry and store them in a jar for future use. Sage is excellent for flavoring meat dishes and dressings.

Tarragon is bushy, with long, droopy branches and long, narrow leaves, very green and twisty, a bit larger than the leaves of rosemary. It can be grown from seed, but most people prefer to buy a pot already started. It is a native of Russia.

Rosemary

Sage

Tarragon

Use young, tender leaves in cooking fish or chicken and in salads. To make tarragon vinegar, pick some leaves and tips of stems; wash, drain, and put them into a glass. Cover them with some wine vinegar and let them steep for a week. Strain, and use that vinegar to flavor more vinegar.

Thyme can be grown from seed, but plant nurseries grow it from root division. It has tiny leaves that are almost round and is a dusty green in color. It grows like a ground cover and makes a plant from two to ten inches tall. It likes sun and not too much water. Give it good drainage. Cut it back severely after flowering. It is kin to mint and has pale purple flowers.

Thyme is a very strong herb. Use it sparingly in sauces, meats, vegetables, baked beans, stuffing, and soups.

CHAPTER 6

Care and Culture
of Blooming Bulbs

Bulbs have been known and loved for thousands of years. They were grown indoors by the Romans, Egyptians, and Indians. In the year 1500, Carpaccio painted Saint Ursula with a pot of flowering bulbs. Sir Thomas More grew bulbs indoors in "flint tumbler glasses and glass bosoms."

Something To Talk About

Learning about Bulbs

Talk about bulbs as living organisms. They drink, eat, rest, and breathe. Discuss the ways in which they are different from other plants because they are their own food storehouses. They already have embryo flowers inside them ready to come up, or they are reservoirs of food for the plant until it can make its own roots and leaves.

Bulbs bloom and the foliage produces food that is stored in the bulb. Then they rest. The more leaves, the more food that will be stored for the next year's blooming. That is why the leaves of a bulb should never be cut off after flowering. If the bulb is to be stored for use next year, or planted outdoors, the leaves should be allowed to mature, turn brown or yellow, and die down. Until they do this the plant should be fed and watered.

Bulbs have to have a long dormant or rest period during which they should be kept in the dark, in temperatures not higher than forty or fifty degrees. This process is often not possible in an apartment or a home without a cool cellar, porch, or patio. Luckily it is now possible to buy bulbs that have already been given this dormant period in the plant nursery before they are sold. Such bulbs are called "prepared." Always ask for prepared bulbs if space and temperature make it impossible to provide the bulbs with a long, cool rest period.

Talk about the importance of always buying top-quality bulbs; not necessarily the largest, but large and firm. Never buy bulbs that look spotty or feel mushy. Treat bulbs gently. They bruise easily and are quite delicate. Buy bulbs from a reputable dealer. Buy early in the season and buy early-blooming varieties for indoor growing.

Bulbs, since they are storehouses of food, will grow and bloom in water or in soil. If grown in water, the bulb cannot replenish its food supply for next year's blooming. These bulbs must be discarded after flowering or planted outdoors to make new food. The exception to this is the paperwhite narcissus, which completely exhausts itself in water and should be discarded after flowering.

Discuss growing bulbs in water and how to do it. Fill a bowl, pot, pan, tureen, or other container without drainage holes, with wet sphagnum moss, moist sand, or pebbles in water. Sphagnum moss should be soaked a full day ahead. Put it in a cloth bag and weight it down so that the moss will absorb all the water it can hold. It takes time for this to happen.

Then lightly press the bulbs down into the moss and cover them up to their necks with more wet moss. Keep them moist at all times. Bulbs require moisture to grow. In using pebbles make sure the bulbs are firmly anchored in the container. They have a tendency to thrust themselves out. In moist sand bury the bulbs up to their necks.

Talk about growing bulbs in soil, and pot some. Use a mixture of good potting soil, peat moss, and sand. Plant the bulbs up to their necks. A big bulb can have its own pot, but several small bulbs can share the same pot. Bowls two inches deep are large enough for small bulbs like scillas or snowdrops, both of which are shallow-rooted, but not deep enough for hyacinths, narcissus, or crocus. They need bowls that are three and a half or four inches deep. Do not press down hard on bulbs when planting. They can be crushed.

Bulbs look best when the same variety is planted together, so that they will all be about the same height and will make a better show of color when blooming. Make weekly plantings for a long succession of flowering.

Talk about which bulbs to plant. Try the easiest ones first. Narcissus, hyacinths, scillas, and crocus are not only among the prettiest, they are also among the easiest. Tulips are much more difficult. So are freesias and cyclamen.

Keep the bowls moist but not soggy. As the plants grow turn the containers so that the plants will grow straight. When they bloom keep them out of the sun. The cooler they are, the longer the blooms will last.

Something To Do

After talking and learning about bulbs, the next step is to grow them! Start growing some of the favorites.

Learning about Favorite Bulbs

The narcissus is a great favorite for indoor growing. The pretty paperwhite narcissus is one of the most popular. It flowers in about a month in soil or in water with moss, sand, or pebbles. Plant it with its neck half-exposed, water it, put it in a dark place for rooting, then bring it to the light. When grown in water, the bulbs will never regain their strength. Throw them out after flowering.

Other varieties of narcissus, sometimes called daffodils or jonquils, grow easily in soil or water. Buy bulbs that have two

Narcissus Bulb   **Paperwhite Narcissus**

or more growing points, or noses. Each will produce flowers. Plant them with noses exposed, two inches apart. Keep in a dark place until growth starts, then introduce them to the light. Do not try to hurry daffodils. Keep them cool and moist, and give them light. If grown in soil, let the foliage die down naturally. Then let the soil in the pot dry out completely before removing the bulb for storage.

Notice the three petals and three sepals that make the perianth of the daffodil. The corona is the trumpet, crown, cup, eye, or center, depending upon the variety. Notice the variations in color among the different varieties. Some are shades of yellow, some buffy-pink, white, red-cupped, yellow-cupped. Some are double. Smell them. Daffodils are fragrant. Touch the flowers. Notice how crisp they feel.

Hyacinths give the longest flowering show of any bulb. Yellow hyacinths are the hardest to grow, blue the easiest. Try some of the new miniatures, planting several close together in one pot. Plant hyacinths every two weeks for a succession of

Hyacinth

blooms. Keep the bowl in a cool, dark closet or other similar place, perhaps in a box under the bed in a cool bedroom, until growth starts. Notice how the bud comes up along with the leaves. Watch them carefully and when the flower buds are well out of the neck of the bulb, bring it into the light. It needs lots of light. If two flower shoots appear, cut one off. The remaining one will grow larger. Keep moist but do not over-water. When the flowering is over let the foliage die down. Then store the bulb in a cool, dry place for next year, plant it outdoors, or give it to a friend with a garden.

Hyacinths, like paperwhite narcissus, grow well in water. Use the special hyacinth glass sold by florists and garden centers. The big bulb fits nicely into the top of such a glass. Fill the bottom with water up to the base of the bulb. Use rain water if possible. Place the glass with the bulb in a cool, dark place until the roots develop. Add water to the glass when necessary. Bring it out into bright light when the flower bud is well up. If the flower should start to bloom when the leaves are still small, put a cone of paper over the plant, leaving an opening at the top for light. The plant will grow upward toward the light.

Hyacinths have an interesting legend. Apollo, the god of the sun, invited a mortal youth, Hyacinthus, to visit his court. After a day of sight-seeing, listening to music, and eating the food of the gods, Apollo challenged the youth to a game of discus throwing. Zephyr, the East wind, was jealous of the attention Apollo was giving the youth, so he tried to blow the youth's discus off course. Hyacinthus had calculated the strength of the wind, however, took very careful aim, and made a good high score. Then Zephyr blew Apollo's discus out of course so that it hit Hyacinthus on the forehead and killed him.

Apollo was greatly saddened. In memory of his mortal friend he caused the blood from Hyacinthus' wound to change into a path of beautiful flowers, which he named hyacinths.

The *crocus* is one of the gayest and earliest of the bulbs. Buy purple, blue, white, or lavender ones. Yellow ones will not bloom indoors.

Plant the bulbs in October or November in light, sandy, well-drained soil or in a bowl of moist sphagnum moss or pebbles. Put them in a cool, dry place until roots form. Then bring them into bright light, but keep them in a cool room. Crocuses do not like heat. Bring them into a warm room for decoration when they are in bloom, but never let them dry out. Keep them out of the sun when blooming. Let the leaves die down after flowering; then replant them in the garden for next spring's blooming. The corm will grow a new corm on top of the old.

Lily of the valley is one of the sweetest smelling of all the bulbs, and one of the prettiest. It grows from fleshy stems called rhizomes, or pips. Florists sell already planted rhizomes and they are easy to grow. Just do not over-water. Throw them out when they have finished blooming. These prepared rhizomes will not bloom again.

For permanent rhizomes, buy them or get them from a neighbor's garden. Refrigerate them in a plastic bag with sphagnum moss for successive plantings.

Crocus Bulbs   **Crocus Flowers**

They can be planted in sphagnum moss, peat moss, or potting soil. Let their noses show. Water the container and put it in a warm, dark, airy place where the temperature is sixty to seventy degrees. Place a bowl of water nearby to provide extra humidity. When the shoots are two to three inches tall, move them gradually into the light, but keep them shaded until they are five or six inches high. Give them no sun. After flowering, plant outdoors or give the pips to someone with an outdoor garden. They will bloom the next year.

Scillas are easy to grow, too. They have very bright blue flowers and are very pretty. Plant a number of them close together for a good showing. Plant them an inch deep and an inch apart, from August to November for successive flowerings.

Keep the bowl of scilla bulbs in a cool, dark room until growth starts. Then bring them into a bright, sunny place, but one that is cool. Try growing scillas also in moist sphagnum moss or in a bowl of pebbles, like narcissus.

The *amaryllis* is the most spectacular of all the bulbs. Children enjoy it because the bulb is so large and because once it starts to grow, they can almost *see* it grow. Its flowers are very large, on a tall stem, and come in gorgeous colors—red, pink, orange, white, purple, and even striped! The bulbs are expensive but make a show that is worth the money. Buy a prepared bulb. If planted in early November it will blossom in time for Christmas.

The pot for an amaryllis should be quite small for the size of the bulb. Allow about an inch from the edge of the pot to the bulb. Plant the bulb like a "sitting duck", about one-half to two-thirds out of the soil. The soil should be potting soil plus sharp sand.

The bulb will root in a dark place in six to eight weeks.

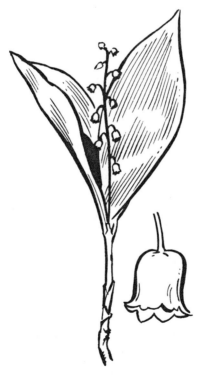

Lily of the Valley

Scilla

Do not give it much water until the leaves and flower bud appear. Then put it in the sun, turning it daily to keep the flower stem growing straight, and water it more at this time.

After it flowers, continue to feed and water it to encourage good root growth. Keep it growing all summer. In the fall, stop watering it. Store the pot in a cool, dry place. The leaves may or may not die back. In January bring it out into the sun and warmth again, watering it a bit. Do not re-pot. Just add a little fresh soil at the top after removing about an inch of the old. Amaryllis does not like to be transplanted.

Learning about Special Bulb Projects

Raising favorite bulbs is fun for children because once the rooting time is over, bulbs grow rapidly and flower well. For even more fun, try a few special projects:

Bulbs-in-a-sponge. Punch holes or cut small openings in a sponge. Insert a number of small bulbs, perhaps grape hyacinths or crocus. Soak the sponge thoroughly in water and hang it in a string bag, such as an onion bag, for two or three weeks in a cool, dark place. The bulbs will make roots. Take the sponge out of the bag, put it in a saucer, or hang it up by a string. Keep the sponge moist. The bulbs will grow and flower.

Crocus moss ball. Something like the sponge project. Make a ball out of wet sphagnum moss. Then add some crocus bulbs, covering them with more moss. Bind the moss into a big, loose ball with a string. Leave a length of string for hanging the ball up.

Soak it thoroughly in water and hang it in a cool, dark place. Watch for signs of growing, then soak the ball again. Put a pan under it to catch the drippings. When growth has clearly begun, hang the ball in a sunny window, keep it moist, and see what happens.

Baby or miniature daffodils are child-size, dainty replicas of their relatives, the big trumpets. They make delightful projects or gifts for children or invalids. Grow them in moist sphagnum moss or in soil, keeping them in a cool, dark place until they sprout. They are very thirsty, so keep them well-watered. Place the bowl or pot where the little flowers can be seen at close range. They will last longer in a cool room.

The autumn crocus is not really a crocus, although it looks like one. It is a strange little bulb. It will bloom without soil or water when its fall blooming time has come. Put a bulb in a low vase or saucer on a windowsill. The little bulb will bloom just like that, without soil or water!

CHAPTER 7

Looking Gift Plants in the Pot

One good way of arousing and sharing interest in indoor gardening is through the care of gift plants. Raising plants from seeds and cuttings and using them as gifts to friends and neighbors is one side of this. Another is to use the pleasure and excitement of getting a beautiful plant as a gift to arouse interest in the way of growth and its proper care to keep the plant healthy and happy.

Gift plants are often sent to churches, institutions, clubrooms, and other places where children can be of help in caring for them. They are welcome gifts that decorate such areas and make them look more hospitable. Children often learn the proper care of such gifts by child-adult discussions and work in the home.

Something To Talk About

Making a point of sharing the beauty of the plant is an important first step. Noticing and pointing out the colors of the leaves and flowers, touching the petals, smelling the fragrance, looking at the textures and shapes of the leaves are all simple ways of awakening a child's interest in what might otherwise be regarded as merely an adult's gift, of no special concern to him.

As soon as the plant arrives give the child the excitement of opening the wrappings. Admire the plant together. Hold the plant up and ask the child to check the bottom. Usually this will be covered with heavy foil. Poke holes in the foil and look to see if the pot has drainage holes.

Talk about why the gift plant needs extra water as soon as it arrives. Remind the child that the plant has left the moist plant nursery or florist shop and its leaves may have lost some of their moisture. Talk about using tepid water—because cold water might shock the roots, just as a cold shower shocks a person. Under a shock the plant might drop its leaves or flowers. If the water has been treated with chlorine it should sit a while before using, to get rid of the chemical.

If the plant does not come with a saucer, the child can find one for it. Help him to pick out a good, big one, deep enough for a layer of pebbles in the bottom for the plant to stand on. The water in the bottom of the saucer will add humidity to the air around the plant. Most plants cannot stand wet feet for very long, but they need more humidity than the average home or apartment can provide.

Learning Where to Place the Gift Plant

If the plant is to provide more than just a few day's enjoyment, give some thought about where it should be placed. Like pets, plants need special places in the home. Gift plants, especially flowering or fruiting ones, can be very fussy. Many of them require a cool temperature of sixty to sixty-five degrees—a bit cool for many people. If the room has to be as warm as seventy degrees, be sure to increase the humidity.

All plants dislike drafts. Many will drop their leaves, flowers, or fruit if placed near an open door or in line with an electric fan or heater. Encourage the child to look over the room carefully for such hazards.

Most flowering plants like light, but their flowers will last longer if they are not in the direct sun. Which window will provide light but not sun?

Almost all flowers, with the exception of cactus, cannot stand dry heat. Talk about the danger of placing a plant on a radiator unless it has been completely insulated with a piece of asbestos or other fiber. Even then, place the pot in a saucer or tray in which a layer of pebbles or a block of wood is placed to keep the pot above the level of water in the container.

Plants cannot stand extremes of cold. A windowbox or windowsill may be pleasantly warm in the daytime, but almost freezing during a cold night. Suggest that the child either move the plant at night or put several layers of newspapers between it and the window.

Like most people, plants like company. Work together to group the plants on a large tray, stand, table, or other place. Suggest that plants of different heights and flowers of different colors can make a pleasant grouping.

Learning about After-Care of Gift Plants

One important rule to learn and practice together is this: water, but don't overwater. Plants' roots must have air. If they are waterlogged they may rot. Talk about never letting most plants dry out completely. Once in a while the child can dunk the plant, pot and all, into water up over the top and let the plant get thoroughly soaked. Then it should drain well, to get rid of excess water.

Point out that plants breathe through the pores on their leaves, called stomata. The child can keep the leaves clean by spraying them, or wiping them with a damp cloth. If the leaves are curly or fuzzy, dust them with a soft brush.

Remind the child to fertilize the plant about once a month, unless it is "resting." Encourage him to read the directions carefully and then to use *less* than the regular dosage. Better to use too little than too much.

In the summer many gift plants profit by being put out on a terrace, porch, patio, or garden, if the home has any of these. Move them out gradually, a few hours a day at first. Place them where they will be protected from rain, sun, and wind. They will need more water outdoors than they did indoors. If it is not possible to take the houseplants outdoors, then make sure that the plants are protected from sun that may be too hot, and from cold breezes from electric fans or air conditioners.

Something To Do

Learning about Special Gift Plants

Talk about the fact that plants, like people and pets, vary widely in their special needs. A sunny window will make one thrive and another die. One plant can stand dim light, another needs bright light. Some plants grow best in cool rooms, others like warmth. Learn together what various gift plants are like and what they need in the way of special care. The following are among those most often given or received as gifts:

Azaleas. These lovely plants get their name from the Greek word meaning "dry" because they are supposed to grow on dry soil. Gift azaleas usually belong to one of two types. The Kurume type is a shrubby, little bush-like plant with many stems coming up from the ground. It arrives covered with pretty little flowers, often in shades of pink, but sometimes white. This type of azalea is quite hardy. Where there is a garden and weather permitting, it can be transplanted outdoors.

The second type is called Indica. If the gift azalea has one rather thick stem almost like a small tree, with its leaves and flowers making a mound above the stem, the azalea is probably an Indica. Its flowers are larger and more ruffly than the other. It does not thrive outdoors north of Washington, D.C.

Azaleas need a rest period of about a month or so in the late summer and cool fall, in a place where the temperature ranges from forty to fifty degrees. A cold bedroom, an outside windowbox, or other cool place will do. Keep the plant moist and feed it once a month. By late fall, tiny buds should start forming. Bring it into a cool room and give it light. Do not water it very much at this period and do not fertilize it. Let it rest. In January give it some sun if possible, water it well, and feed it. It should present another display of beautiful flowers.

Azaleas like to be cool. They do best in a room with a temperature of around sixty. Keep the soil moist when the plant is resting.

Study the gift azalea. Is it the Kurume or the Indica type? Does it have one main stem, or many? Are the flowers rather small, or quite large and ruffly? Look at the leaves. Note that they are evergreen. The azalea belongs to the same big family as the rhododendrons.

If possible, go together to find a wild azalea in the woods. In the Northeast it is called pinkster. In some other areas it is called wild honeysuckle. Can you see why? Look at the shape of the pink flowers and compare them with a honeysuckle flower. In the southern mountains there is a yellow variety like a golden flame in the woods. If the family or group takes a trip to the Blue Ridge Mountains or the Great Smokies, look for it in the spring.

Bulbs (see Chapter 6 for information about specific bulbs). Gift pots or bowls of daffodils, hyacinths, tulips, and other spring flowers are welcome gifts, but they soon become unsightly when they have finished flowering. If the flowers are growing in soil when they arrive, water them thoroughly, and then again every time the soil seems at all dry. Bulbs take a lot of water.

When flowering is over, cut off the flowering stems, but not the leaves. They must make food for next year's bloom. Water and fertilize the plants. When the leaves turn yellow and flabby reduce the water and let the plant rest. Eventually the pot will dry out. When this happens take the bulbs out and plant them in the garden or give them to someone with a garden. They will grow again, although not all will bloom the next year.

If the bulbs are growing in water, held down by pebbles, make sure that the water reaches the roots but does not cover the bulbs. When the flowering is over, these water-grown bulbs seldom make enough food to bloom again. In the case of paperwhite narcissus they never will. Enjoy them while they last; then discard them.

Flowering bulbs make lovely and welcome gifts for a child to raise and send to relatives, to his church, to friends in the hospital, or to Mother on Mother's Day. Encourage the child to write a little note to send with the gift, giving instructions on caring for it.

Christmas Pepper (Capsicum frutescens). This spectacular plant belongs to the same family as the lowly potato. It is often given as a Christmas gift because of its red fruits and green leaves, but it appears in florists' windows during other seasons as well.

Notice how the little peppers stand up among the foliage. As they ripen they change color several times, sometimes from white to red, sometimes from green to purple to red. They are not edible.

Be very careful where this plant is placed. It is *very* fussy about drafts, and very often it will drop all its little peppers. It likes a room with a temperature from sixty to sixty-five degrees. Always keep it moist. It likes light, but not direct sun.

If it is happy in the room, it will keep on "peppering" until February. Save some of the peppers and plant the seeds in April or May. When the seedlings have made their second or third pairs of leaves, transplant each to a small pot. They will grow nicely and can be transplanted to a larger pot in time to make fall or winter gifts. They are tender and cannot stand cold weather. Keep them out of cold, drafty windows on winter nights.

Chrysanthemums. Very few flowers can boast of as long and honorable a history. In China, more than five hundred years before Confucius, they were regarded as symbols of perfection. The Chinese knew and loved them more than two hundred years before they were imported into Japan, where they became the royal flower. They were introduced into Europe in the seventeenth century and into America in the eighteenth century.

When the gift pot of chrysanthemums arrives, keep it out of the sun and keep it watered. The blooms should last for weeks. When flowering is over, ask the child to cut the plant down to within four inches of the pot, put it in a light window, and water it just enough to keep it alive. Then he can watch for new foliage to develop.

The formation of flowers on a chrysanthemum is based upon the amount of light the plant gets. These plants are forced to bloom out of season by being shaded with slats or cloth. That is why chrysanthemums are available in bloom at all seasons of the year.

Look at the "petals" of a chrysanthemum flower. Notice that on the outer edge is a row of flat, elongated "petals" which are really "ray" flowers. In the center look for the "disk" flowers, shorter and more compact. Pull out a ray and a disk flower and compare them. The big "football mum" is made up mostly of ray flowers. The "spoon" and the "spider" mums are mostly disk flowers. The former is an exotic plant with long, curved-in petal-like flowers. The latter has feathery, long-petaled blooms that move very gracefully.

The two kinds of mums most often used as gift plants are the tall plants covered with fairly small, compact heads of flowers called "button" mums, and the low, bushy, compact plants literally covered with small heads of flowers, called "cushion" mums.

Cinerarias (Senecio cruentus). If the gift plant looks like a big mound of daisies, it is likely to be a cineraria. These flowers come in a wide variety of colors and color combinations and are very pretty.

This plant is an annual. It will fade and die after its blooming time is over. When this happens do not try to save it. Enjoy its beauty—and then discard it.

The cineraria likes light, a temperature around sixty-five degrees, and fresh air. Keep it moist but not soggy.

Citrus Plants (see Chapter 4 for growing them from seed). Small orange, lemon, tangerine, and kumquat trees are popular gift plants. They range from about fifteen inches to four feet in height, although they don't usually get so tall. They are pretty little trees with small, white, fragrant flowers and bright-colored fruit, sometimes edible, sometimes not. The foliage is shiny green, broadleaved, and evergreen. The plants grow slowly, live a long time, and are quite decorative.

These citrus plants like a cool room between fifty and sixty-five degrees. They like sun or filtered light in the spring and summer.

Select a sunny window for the plant. Spray the foliage once a week to provide humidity and to keep the leaves clean. Cut down on water on the dark days of winter. At other times, water moderately, letting the plant get almost dry between waterings. Encourage the child to keep an eye open for any insects; destroy them when found. Note how spiny a lemon tree can be. Enjoy the fragrant flowers. Taste the fruit. Is it good, bitter, or insipid?

Work together to pollinate the flowers so that the plant will produce fruit. Give a child a soft watercolor brush or a bit of cotton on a toothpick. He can brush some of the pollen from the stamens of one flower onto the pistils of another. Then he can watch to see if his pollination has been successful. If the plant sets fruit, it was!

Cyclamens. A cyclamen plant in full flower is a dazzling sight. The whole plant seems to have a flock of bright butterflies hovering over it. Notice the beautiful, reflexed flowers in many lovely colors—white, pink, red, and other shades. It is one of the loveliest of gift flowers, and one of the hardest to grow. The reason for this is that cyclamens are raised from bulbs in very cool greenhouses where the temperature is always kept around sixty degrees, a bit chilly for family living. They arrive looking so lovely, full of flowers, and with dozens of promising buds under the leaves. In many, many cases these buds do not survive, and the stems of the leaves and flowers get sticky and mushy and have to be pulled off. Anyone who can keep a cyclamen alive and happy in the average overheated home has quite a green thumb. These plants have to be pampered. Keep them moist but not soggy, and above all *keep them cool.*

Easter Lilies. When one of these stately symbols of purity arrives as a gift, put it in as cool a place as possible. It will last much longer. Water the plant whenever the top soil feels a bit dry.

When the lily stops blooming cut off the flowerstalk but not the leaves. Put the pot in a sunny place and keep it alive and happy until spring planting time. Then take the bulb out of the pot and transplant it into the garden. It may bloom again in August or September. If there isn't a garden, let the lily live as long as it will in the pot. When its leaves get yellow and flabby, stop all watering and let the plant dry out completely. It will be unsightly, so hide it behind other plants. When all the leaves have withered, take the bulb out of the pot, store it in a cool, dry place for next year, or give it to a friend who has a garden.

Gardenias. A gardenia plant is one of the queens of shrubbery. It has glossy evergreen leaves, and its white, very fragrant flowers are among the best-loved.

Sometimes a gardenia plant disappoints its caretaker by dropping all its flowerbuds. It is very definite in its requirements for flowering. First of all, it must have a fairly cool, even temperature of sixty to seventy degrees, and not less than fifty-five degrees at night. If the temperature goes over seventy degrees the plant is not likely to open its buds. It needs sun at least part of the day and it needs humidity. It likes fresh air and space around it. Do not crowd it in with other plants. Feed it monthly with a fertilizer for acid soil.

Prune the plant to keep it shapely. Cut back the leafy terminal branches. Encourage the child to try to root some of these in a mixture of moist sand and peat moss. Keep the cuttings covered with a glass while rooting to conserve humidity. Pot the little plants when they are quite small. Gardenias do not like to be transplanted once they are established. The little plants will grow to gift size very nicely.

Gloxinias. If the gift plant has fleshy, fairly large leaves and velvety, trumpet-shaped flowers, sometimes double, in a wide variety of colors and color combinations, it is likely to be a gloxinia, a cousin to the African violets. Its flowers can be purple, red, white, or combinations of these. Feel them. They are like velvet. See Chapter 9 for their care and culture.

Hydrangeas. A potted hydrangea is a spectacular gift plant. The huge blue or pink flower clusters almost hide the leaves. For fun start to count the flowers in any one cluster!

The first and most important thing to do with a gift hydrangea is to *soak* it. Water it thoroughly, then drain off the excess water. Make sure the pot and its foil covering have drainage holes. Soak the plant every day. It needs these thorough wettings to maintain those enormous trusses of flowers.

To make the plant bloom next year cut it down to within four inches of the pot after it has finished blooming. Re-pot it into a larger pot, adding at least half peat moss to the potting mixture to provide acidity Feed and water the plant all summer. Store it in early winter in a cool place with a temperature from thirty-five to fifty degrees, and water it occasionally. Hydrangeas will not bloom unless they are exposed to temperatures below fifty degrees for six weeks. Use an outside flowerbox, terrace, porch, patio, garage, cellar, or other cold place for this period.

Around January bring the plant into the light, put it in a cool window, and gradually increase the watering. Feed it every two weeks.

Jerusalem Cherry (Solanum pseudo-capsicum). This festive plant, so gay with its myriad small red fruits, is a favorite Christmas gift. It belongs to the same general family as the Christmas Pepper. Treat it the same way.

If the plant refuses to be happy in the home and persists in losing its little red "cherries" (they are not edible), encourage the child to try growing them from seed. In February, or when a cherry seems ripe, take its seeds and sow them in a pot or flat of moist, sandy soil. They germinate easily. When the second pair of leaves has formed, transplant the seedlings into little pots. These little plants should develop flowers in time for the fruits to ripen for the Christmas season, and the child will have gift-size plants for friends and relatives.

Kalanchoe (Kalanchoe blossfeldiana). This little gift plant with fleshy leaves and covered with tiny red flowers is in every florist's windows around Christmas. Unlike most gift plants it does not require much water because it belongs to the family of succulents. Try grouping several pots of kalanchoes together. They will make a very gay and festive spot in a room.

The kalanchoe likes a cool temperature, but it also likes sunlight; so be careful that the sunlight is not too hot.

Try propagating little kalanchoes for next Christmas. They start as easily as African violets and in the same ways. Just snip off a leaf with an inch of stem and insert it into a starting mixture of moist sand, vermiculite, potting soil, or such. Or insert half of the leaf itself into the mixture. Cover the pot or flat with glass or plastic to preserve moisture. Small leaves will start forming after the stem or leaf has rooted. When the new plant is large enough to handle, transplant it into a four-inch pot, water it only moderately, keep it cool, and give it light. As it grows it may need to be re-potted into the next size pot. It should be gift-size by the following Christmas.

Poinsettia (Euphorbia pulcherrima). This gorgeous gift plant, called *Flor de Pascuas* or Flower of Christmas in Mexico, is regarded as just that by everyone. Churches bank their altars with them. Office buildings deck their windows. They are favorite Christmas gifts.

The most popular variety has big red "flowers" (really bracts). The real flowers are in the center; see if you can find them.

Poinsettias are tropical. They like high humidity, a temperature from sixty to seventy degrees, and bright light or a few hours of sun. They hate chills and drafts. If they are not happy where they are placed, they will drop their leaves, or the leaves will turn yellow. If they are happy they will bloom for six weeks or more.

Some people use poinsettias as foliage plants after the flowers are over, and then discard the plant because it takes effort to preserve it for another year.

It *can* be carried over, however, by learning about its growing habits and giving it the sort of care it needs. When the flowers stop blooming and the leaves drop off, give those barren-looking stems less and less water until the soil is almost dry and most of the leaves are off. Then store the pot in a cool place with a temperature from fifty-five to sixty-five degrees. The place can be dark or light. A closet, windowbox, garage, porch, or other place will do, provided the temperature is right.

When the weather gets warm cut those rangy stems off to within four inches of the pot. Re-pot them, using fresh potting soil. Water well, and feed once a month during the summer. Prune the stems to make the plant more compact, but stop pruning in mid-summer. This pruning is necessary for flower production.

The poinsettia needs dark nights to set its buds. Keep it in a room that is not lighted at night, or see that it is well shaded from any night light. Be very careful of chills and drafts. Given such tender loving care, the poinsettia will re-flower for your Christmas pleasure.

Encourage the child to try to propagate poinsettias. When pruning the plants, save pieces of stem six to eight inches long, cut from the top of a stem. He can insert these slips four inches deep in moist sand, vermiculite, or other rooting material. Cover the slips with glass or plastic to preserve humidity. When the cuttings root and new plants form, he can pot the little plants. Treat them well, keep them happy, and there will be a number of gift plants for his Christmas giving.

CHAPTER 8

Living Room Foliage: Tropical Plants in the Home

Ever since those far-away days when many homes had their own conservatories, solariums, big bay windows, and sometimes their own greenhouses, people of all ages have enjoyed plants with interesting and beautiful foliage. Those were the days before central heating. Room temperatures were likely to be lower, humidity higher, than in today's homes and apartments. Houses were set farther apart and had more sun and air. Today's blocks of houses and high-rise apartments bring all sorts of problems to both plants and people—but they still manage to live together.

The young gardener of today will find that plants grown for their foliage are easier to grow under adverse circumstances than are the flowering plants, many of which demand at least four hours of sun a day and may be finicky about humidity and temperature. (Foliage plants have flowers, too, but they are usually insignificant in comparison with the leaves.)

Something To Talk About

Many of the modern foliage plants are so new that they do not as yet have pet or regional names. They come from all over the world. Discuss the influence of the airplane in bringing new species from one country to another. Those plants from the tropical rain forests of Central and South America are very popular because in their native habitat they grow under tall trees and so need only filtered light, making them useful for dark city apartments, rooms with inadequate light, or for dark corners of rooms. Many are heat tolerant and can even stand dry air, although they will thrive better if given more care.

Visit the lobbies of big office buildings in the city. Look into the windows and malls along the streets. The chances are that you will discover many interesting foliage plants being used for decoration. This is a good way to get acquainted with them. Learn to identify them by name and method of growth. Some may be plastic plants, but they can be very realistic.

Learning How to Choose Foliage Plants

Foliage plants, depending upon their scarcity and size, are often quite expensive, especially for full-grown plants. Try to buy young plants, cheaper and more fun to watch as they mature. Go together to plant nurseries, botanical gardens, florists' shops, and the indoor gardens of office buildings. Check plant catalogs. Ask questions. Note the relative heights of various species. Observe their method of growth. Do they grow straight up, like the palms, or are they bushy and compact? Are they small enough to use on a coffee table? Will they make a good room divider? Is the foliage handsome? Do you both admire the plant?

Note the different textures of the leaves. Some have thin, silky leaves; others have heavy, rubbery ones. Some leaves are like velvet, others like satin. Note the varying *sizes* of the leaves. Some are enormous, others less than an inch long.

Compare their colors. Foliage plants are not just all green. Their greens include every shade and variation, from the very pale to almost black. But what makes foliage plants so fascinating is their wide variations of color. Some, like caladiums, are paper-white. Others are purple, yellow, red, pink, brown, orange. Some plants have several colors in each leaf. Some have stripes, some blotches, some dots, some veins of a different color.

Note their mature size. Will they be too tall, too wide, too spreading when they are mature? Would you buy a puppy without having any idea how big he might be when he grows up?

Learning Where to Place Foliage Plants

Notice where various foliage plants are placed in the plant nursery or botanical garden. Read about their culture in plant catalogs. Can you provide the necessary care? Will the plant be able to live happily where you want to put it? Can it stand the sun from a south window? the dark corner of the room? Will it make a pleasant grouping with the other plants? Is it too heavy to move around easily? Can it be too easily knocked over by the children? Talk it over. Plants, like pets, should fit into family life. They need not be limited to any one room or section of the house. Any room, including the bathroom, can look more livable with the right plant in it. And every member of the family, young or old, can enjoy a plant in his or her room.

Something To Do

Learning How to Care for Foliage Plants

Caring for foliage plants is closely related to where they are placed. Learn which ones need direct sun or filtered sun. Which need good light, which can stand dim light.

Find out by inquiry, observation, and reading, which ones need heavy watering, which can go longer without water. Check their temperature requirements. Some plants can stand a wide variation. Others are fussy about heat. Some flourish in a warm room, others prefer a cool one.

All plants, except for cacti and certain succulents, do best where there is adequate humidity. Work out ways to supply this. A wet bath towel on a warm radiator will raise the humidity in a room. Water simmering on a stove will do the same. A bowl or pan of water hidden behind a group of plants will provide them with extra moisture. Putting a plant into a larger container on a layer of pebbles or a block of wood, and stuffing the spaces between with moist sphagnum moss will help keep it moist. A mist spray on the leaves and in the air around the plants will raise the humidity. So will a room humidifier—and the family will also benefit.

Plants, like people and pets, need food. Some need fertilizing once a month, some twice a month. As a good general rule, use *less* than the directions call for. Always make sure that the soil around the plant is moist before fertilizing it, so that the roots will not get too strong a dose. Keep the surface of the soil soft and loose by digging it lightly with an old fork whenever it seems caked. This helps the roots to get air, and the soil to absorb moisture.

Also like people and pets, plants *grow*. They outgrow their pots. A general rule of thumb is that an upright plant should not be more than six times as tall as the pot is wide. Most foliage plants will not need re-potting for about a year after purchase. Use the next size pot, based on the diameter of the pot. Provide good drainage. Use a crock (piece of broken clay pot) humped over the drainage hole. Put a thin layer of sand, sphagnum moss, or pebbles in the bottom before adding the potting soil.

Learning about Special Foliage Plants

The plants given below are only a sampling of wonderful and interesting foliage plants available for indoor gardening. Practice using their names, both nicknames and botanical. Decide which will be the nicest to try to grow. Divide responsibility with the child. Let him feel that the plants are his and that he is important to them.

Arrowhead (Syngonium or *Nephthytis).* Its leaves are large, usually arrow-shaped, on long stems. This plant starts off by growing upright, but as it gets taller notice how it starts to trail or climb. When this happens, give it a slab of bark to climb up.

When the leaves begin to get small or to fall off, cut the arrowhead down to within four inches of the pot. Encourage the child to root the leafy ends in water or moist sand to start new plants.

Arrowheads like direct light but no sun.

Artillery Plant (Pilea). This variety of the *Pileas* is *Pilea microphylla.* It is fernlike, with small, inconspicuous flowers that give the plant its name. These little flowers eject their pollen in tiny puffs like smoke from miniature guns! Make sure that the child gets to see this happen. Another variety, *Pilea cadierei,* is called aluminum plant. It has glossy green leaves prettily mottled with silver. Still another variety, *Pilea involucrata,* has coppery leaves with deep veins. Its flowers are inconspicuous and creamy. Contrast the different varieties. Which is the prettiest?

This plant likes light or part-time sun.

Aspidistra. This plant is known by its botanical name and by many nicknames, such as saloon plant, barbershop plant, and castiron plant, all indicating how hardy it is. Its leaves are a very dark green and they all sprout out of the base. A striped variety is also available.

Its needs are simple: occasional water and a bit of light. Touch its leaves. Are they rubbery? Thick? Rough? Talk about how it got its many nicknames.

Baby's Tears (Helxine). Sometimes called Irish moss, mother-of-thousands, or pollyanna. This is a pretty little creeping plant with a dense mat of tiny green leaves. It is easily propagated. Stick a piece from an old plant into a pot. It will look very dead for days, and then start growing nicely if kept moist. Talk about the reasons for its many names.

This little plant likes warmth, light, moisture and humidity.

Caladium is a foliage plant grown from a tuber. A child will enjoy growing it from scratch. He can plant a tuber in peat moss about an inch and a half deep. The top of the tuber is usually knobby, but don't worry about top or bottom. The tuber will grow even if planted upside down. It likes moist, rich soil after its roots form and the leaves emerge.

Caladium leaves are arrow-shaped and are patterned beautifully in white, pink, or red. Note how exotic they look. Notice also how the veins of each leaf converge to a central point where

Chinese Evergreen

the color intensifies. This plant is a cousin of the huge-leaved "elephant ear" plant, and is a native of South America. It likes semi-shade and moisture.

Chinese Evergreen (Aglaonema). This popular, very hardy plant is a native of China and Borneo. It has dark green, pointed leaves that grow on a thick stem. This plant will grow in either soil or water. It can grow as tall as two feet or be kept low by pruning. Its flowers are like very small calla lilies, whitish, inconspicuous, but interesting.

Aglaonema will tolerate hot rooms and poor light.

Coleus. One of the most popular houseplants because of its leaves, which are as colorful as flowers. They come in gorgeous combinations of gold, red, green, cream, and pink. Coleus is easily grown from seed, and watching the various color combinations in the small plants is fascinating. Leaf cuttings will root in water or moist sand. Most florists and plant nurseries sell many different varieties. Grow your own or choose the ones you think the prettiest.

Coleus needs sun to bring out the leaf colorings. It likes to be moist.

Dieffenbachia (D. amoena). This is the toughest variety of dieffenbachia, with leathery leaves that have white markings along the veins. Touch them. Note the very heavy middle veins in the large leaves. They are typical of this plant. It is a native of Central and South America and will grow several feet tall.

In other varieties of this plant the leaves are mottled, or spotted, or otherwise marked in shades of white, yellow, or green. It makes a spectacular houseplant, tolerant of heat and poor light. Give it a good soaking about once a week. It can be

Dieffenbachia

placed in difficult locations because it is so hardy. It can stand heat and dim light, but try to do better by it.

Dragon Plant (Dracaena). This plant comes from the Congo and Cameroon parts of Africa. It will grow to six feet tall with strange, exotic, twisting branches. The leaves are narrow and spear-like, green or striped. One variety has leaves that are green in the center and dark red at the borders. Note that the leaves grow like the leaves on a cornstalk. It needs constant moisture and fast-draining soil. Never let it dry out. Otherwise it is very hardy.

It likes light but not sun, and will tolerate dim light.

Fiddleleaf Fig (Ficus lyrata). This plant with its very large, shiny, leathery green leaves shaped like a violin and growing on a woody stalk, is a popular foliage plant. It will grow tall but can be kept pruned back. It is very tough, kin to the old-fashioned rubber plant, but its leaves are glossier and longer. The fiddleleaf fig (it has no figs) will drop its leaves if its roots dry out, so keep it moist.

It will tolerate heat and likes direct light but no sun.

Norfolk Island Pine (Araucaria excelsa). Easy to identify because it looks like a Christmas tree—and can be used as one. It comes, however, from the tropical Norfolk Islands in the South Pacific. It is needle-leaved, stiff, and it grows two to four feet tall. Notice that its very symmetrical branches grow in a circle around the trunk. They make lovely shadows on a wall. This plant needs constant moisture and a cool temperature from fifty to seventy degrees. It grows slowly, lives a long time, and is quite tolerant of adverse conditions, but try to treat it right.

It is hardy, likes light, but will tolerate dim light.

Palms (Palmaceae) come in all sizes, from dainty little ones suitable for coffee tables to tall ones needing heavy tubs. Notice the characteristic crown of leaves at the top of the trunk. The lady palm has large, coarse leaves. The dainty date palm comes from India. All palms grow slowly. Keep them moist. Read about them in an encyclopedia. They have played a big part in the history of many countries.

They are very hardy, and can stand dim light and heat.

Peperomias. These are small, bushy, pretty little plants. They

Dragon Plant

Palm

come in many varieties, each with its own individual coloring and leaf shape. Some are heart-shaped, some oval, some deeply indented, some with green leaves and white stripes. Others have combinations of greens, silvers, dark reds, browns, and whites. They do not like too much water. Let the soil almost dry out between waterings, then give them a good soaking with tepid water.

They can stand hot, dry rooms. They like light but not sun.

Philodendrons. The name comes from the Greek, meaning "tree-loving," because these plants grow under and up trees in the tropics. They are among the most popular of all foliage plants, not only because they are hardy and easy to grow, but also because they come in so many different varieties, sizes, and shapes. Coming from tropical rain forests of Central and South America, many varieties climb; some do not, but all can stand dim, filtered light. They develop thin, dangling aerial roots. Notice them. Do not cut them off. They help to provide food for the plant.

A large variety is sometimes called monstera, or Mexican breadfruit. Its leaves are very large and become deeply split as the plant matures. In the rain forests these split leaves are very useful in helping the plant to survive very heavy rains and high winds. Rain runs off the many leaf points and the wind can blow through.

They are heavy feeders and like rich soil and moisture. Spray the leaves frequently to keep them clean and to provide humidity.

These plants can grow too tall or too long. If they do, cut them back and start new plants. A tip on eye cutting: cut below a leaf joint of the third or fourth leaf from the top. This cutting should be from four to ten inches long. Put the cutting, eye down, into a mixture of soil and peat moss and keep it moist. Notice that these plants have their eye or growth buds *opposite* the crotch, instead of in it like most plants.

Any eye bud laid horizonally or set vertically into a starting mixture will develop a new plant. Try both ways and see which grows faster.

Philodendrons are hardy and can stand dim light, but do best in a good light without sun.

Piggyback Plant (Tolmiea menziesii). This interesting little

Two Varieties of Philodendron

plant gets its name from its habit of carrying new little plants at the base of its leaves, piggyback-like. Children—and adults, too—enjoy taking off the entire leaf, inserting it into a pot of moist sand, and letting the new little plants develop roots. Then they can be potted in soil.

The leaves of this plant are shaped like maple leaves. Compare them with the leaves of a maple tree and see how like they are. They grow straight up the long stems, making the plant look nice and full.

This is one of the few foliage plants native to the United States. It grows wild along the coast of the Northwest.

It likes moisture and cool temperatures. Give it light but not sun.

Pittosporum (P. tobira). This is a handsome evergreen shrub that grows outdoors in the southeast United States. It looks grownup even when it is very small and young. It has a sturdy, woody stem, like a small trunk with tufts of dark green leaves at the top. These leaves fall off in the summer and new ones take their places. The plant has lots of small, white flowers that are very fragrant. These do not bloom until the plant is mature.

Pittosporum likes moist soil and medium light.

Podocarpus is well-known not only as a foliage plant for indoor gardening, but also for its ornamental branches that are sold for cut greens to use alone or with cut flowers. It is an evergreen shrub that grows outdoors in the South, where it is used in foundation plantings around homes, like its cousins, the yews. It has very woody stems that are covered with narrow, needle-like leaves, very dark green. In the spring, flowers that look like tiny pinecones come out on the tips of the branches and drop yellow pollen. Look for the flowers; they are strange. This plant is hardy and slow-growing, but can eventually grow as tall as four feet.

It is quite tolerant. Keep it moist and give it moderate light.

Prayer Plant (Maranta kerchoveana). This Brazilian plant gets its name from the way its leaves turn upward at night and fold together like hands in prayer. This habit makes it interesting to both children and adults.

The leaves are thin, broad, and oval, with rows of dark, chocolate-brown spots on each side of the middle of the leaf. Notice the lovely contrast of colors in the leaves. It is a handsome plant.

Other varieties have blotches of pink, light green, or purple at the top or undersides of the leaves. They are all pretty, bushy plants that do well indoors. They like moist soil. Spray them for added humidity. They like warmth. Give them medium light but no sun.

Rubber Plant (Ficus elastica). A native of India and Malaysia. This variety, so popular years ago, has been largely replaced by the newer variety, *Ficus decora.* This variety has leaves that are wider and more oval, often tinged with bronze. When new leaves emerge they look quite red. Notice how they gradually change to bronzy green. The rubber plants are kin to the fiddle-leaf fig and just as hardy. They can tolerate heat, need moisture, and like direct light but not sun.

Snake Plant (Sansevieria). A popular name for this well-known plant is mother-in-law's tongue, perhaps because of the sharp, spiky tip on each leaf. The whitish or greenish mottling on the leaves gives it its name of snake plant. The leaves are straight, stiff, and upright. Sometimes the plant produces a spike of small white blossoms. It is a native of India and tropical Africa.

Snake Plant

It is practically indestructible. It can stand heat, dryness, dim light, dry air. Do not over-water. Wash the leaves; they get dusty.

Spider Plant (Anthericum). Like the piggyback plant, the spider plant has a strange way of growing new plants. It has narrow, green, white-striped leaves that grow in tufts, and out of these tufts smaller tufts grow at the tips of the branches. These small tufts can be snipped off and rooted for plant replacements. Its flowers are white and inconspicuous.

The spider plant likes moisture and medium light.

Ti Plant (Cordyline terminalis). The name of this plant is pronounced "tea." It is a pretty plant. Its leaves are long and narrow, dark green with red edging. They grow in tufts at the top of single stems. The leaves taper and are about six inches long and two to five inches wide. When new leaves come, around Christmas, they are bright pink. This plant has many varieties with different shadings of color—mostly metallic shades of green, purple, pink, and rose.

The ti plant is expensive when it is full-grown, but small plants are sometimes available.

The ti needs a bit of coddling. Give it lots of moisture and bright light to bring out its delicate coloring.

Umbrella Tree (Schefflera actinophylla). Look at its large, soft green leaves, deeply cut, and see where it probably got its name. One of these leaves would make a good protection in a rainstorm. The leaves are shiny and stay green under very poor conditions. They can stand hot, dry rooms, and they provide an accent for a dreary planter or uninteresting corner. This plant is a native of Australia.

Wash the leaves with a damp cloth once in a while or give the plant a good spraying. It does not need to be kept moist, but should not be allowed to dry out completely.

The umbrella tree is uncomplaining. It can stand hot, dry rooms, and it will live in dim light. Of course the better it is treated, the healthier it will grow.

CHAPTER 9

Enjoying Flower Power at Its Brightest

Flowering plants require much the same care as the foliage plants in Chapter 8. Most of them need adequate moisture and humidity, regular feeding, light, and medium temperatures. Some, like the cactus family, stand drought and heat, but they are exceptions.

Something To Talk About

Discuss the reasons why many flowering plants are more difficult to grow indoors than foliage plants. They usually need four to seven hours of sun a day. Many apartments and homes cannot provide this much sunshine. Foliage plants are mostly tropical in origin and are therefore accustomed to growing under tall trees, in shade or semi-shade.

Nevertheless, many interesting flowering plants can be grown. Some of the popular flowering plants for indoor gardening also come from the tropics. Some are from high altitudes, and some are low-growing, needing less sunshine than the annuals grown outdoors.

Many flowering plants can be started from seed, and when they have made their second leaves, transplanted into the garden border. Zinnias, marigolds, and petunias are great favorites for starting indoors in the spring for later planting outdoors. Pre-planted pans of seeds are available from some nurseries and garden centers, but they cost more and do not provide the fun of do-it-yourself. A green thumb is a dirty thumb, someone has said.

Try growing some of the flowering indoor plants from seed so that the entire life cycle can be watched and enjoyed. Some of the plants grow from tubers; some are propagated easily from leaf or stem cuttings; and some are best bought as young plants from nursery, garden center, or florist.

Something To Do

Learning about Specific Flowering Plants

Many of the following are familiar names. Some may be unfamiliar, but nonetheless suitable for indoor growing. Of these, try raising some by seed, some by cuttings, and some from young plants.

African Violets (Saintpaulia). These plants were known and grown only in conservatories as late as 1930. Since then they have become so popular that there is a very active and large African Violet Society. They were discovered toward the end of the nineteenth century by Baron von St. Paul-Illaire and named after him. They grew wild in Tanganyika, growing among rocks and in crevices, in light and shade, and at altitudes of 50 to 3,000 feet.

Buy a strong, young plant just showing signs of budding. It will stand the transition from nursery or florist shop better than an older plant. Buy it in spring or summer.

Better still, buy some seed from a seed supply company and grow your own plants. It makes an interesting project because the seeds will not run true, and several different varieties of the plants may come up. Sow in the early spring. The seeds are very tiny, so sprinkle them lightly on the top of a good, moist,

Shapes of African Violet Flowers

potting soil mixture that has some peat moss and sand in it to make it porous. These plants like a very light, porous soil. Cover the tiny seeds very lightly with fine sand. Put glass or plastic over the seed flat and shade it with a piece of paper until growth starts. The seeds will be slow to germinate; so be patient.

The seedlings need humidity and light, but not sun. When they have several leaves prick them out carefully, taking care not to break the delicate roots, and pot each in a small pot.

As they grow, African violets often produce a number of little rosettes of leaves from the leaf axils, called side crowns. These will make the plant grow out of shape and should be pinched out with the fingers or with tweezers. Be careful not to remove flower buds. They also grow in leaf axils.

These side shoots can be rooted. They will have only very short stems, so be sure these stems are well-inserted into moist sand. Peg the shoot down with a hairpin if necessary.

African violets are often propagated by leaf cuttings. Snip off a mature leaf from the middle of the plant with about an inch of stem. Let it dry off for an hour or so. Then bury the stem in moist sand or other starting mixture and put a glass over it. A cluster of little plants will start growing in six to eight weeks. Separate these when they are about two inches tall, and pot them. They like to be somewhat potbound, so use a small pot.

Transplant when the roots try to come out of the drainage hole.

A leaf cutting can also be rooted in a glass of water. Cut a piece of cardboard to fit over the top of the glass and cut a hole in it large enough for the stem to fit through. Insert the stem in the hole so that the leaf is supported, but the stem is in the water. It should root in approximately six to eight weeks, whereupon it can be potted.

Water African violets from the top or bottom, but do not let the soil get soggy. Use tepid water and don't let the leaves get wet if the plant is in the sun or a strong light. The water will spot the leaves.

If the leaves of the plant get yellowish or the crown grows too high, the plant may be getting too much sun. If the leaves are a very dark green and the plant will not flower, it may not be getting enough sun or strong light. It likes humidity and a temperature around sixty-five to seventy degrees by day and sixty degrees at night.

Try making your own variety of African violet. It is an interesting project for adult and child to work on together. Open the two yellow, pollen-holding anthers in the middle of a blossom. Dust the pollen on top of the pistil in the center of another flower, using a very fine, soft brush or a bit of cotton on a toothpick. Tie a white bit of thread loosely around that flower so that it can be identified after the petals have fallen. It will take six to seven months for a little seedpod to form. When it is ready to open, snip it off and use the tiny seeds to grow new plants.

Begonias are so generous in their flowering that they are one of the most popular and easiest plants for indoor gardening. They were discovered in the West Indies in 1700 by a monk, Plumier, and named for Michel Begon, the French governor of Santo Domingo. They grow wild in Mexico, Peru, Africa, the Himalayas, and the West Indies. More than 750 varieties are known. The wax begonia is the best known, but the tuberous-rooted is the most spectacular; its flowers are huge and come in a variety of lovely colors. It blooms in the summer, however, and so is usually not raised indoors. It is fine for a shaded porch, patio, or garden. Indoors, the smaller but more bushy wax

Begonia

begonia will bloom profusely all winter.

Begonias can be grown from seed, but the seed is so very fine and dust-like that it is hard to handle. Usually it is simpler to go to a garden center or nursery, look over the many varieties, and pick out the ones you like best. They are inexpensive and rewarding.

Once a plant is growing well, it can be easily propagated by stem cuttings rooted in potting soil, water, or a rooting mixture.

Begonias need rich soil; so fertilize them once a month. They like average temperature and humidity. The soil should be fast-draining to prevent the stems from rotting. In the winter, let the top soil dry before watering.

Examine the flower of a wax begonia. Under the petals is a three-winged ovary called the wings. It is so delicately colored that it looks just like the petals, sometimes a bit deeper in color. Notice the slender stems of the clusters of flowers. Cut them sometimes and use them in flower arrangements.

Bromeliads not only have handsome foliage, but also develop a most spectacular flower stalk rising high above the leaves or crown. The blossoms are an inflorescence. The small individual flowers in it have no petals. It can be blue, purple, rose, pink, yellow, orange, or scarlet, and can last for months. Each plant produces only one flower stalk, but it will send up suckers around the base. The original plant will die, but the suckers can be potted and will usually bloom in one or two years.

The pineapple belongs to the Bromeliad family. In all this family the leaves come from around the base, making a sort of cup or vase around each other. Bromeliad plants are called epiphytic, meaning air plants, and get most of their food from water in those cups or vases. The cups should never be allowed to dry out. Water the plant by keeping the cups filled. Bromeliads can be lightly fertilized by using a bit of liquid fertilizer in the water.

They like a light, porous soil of leafmold, peat moss, and sharp sand. They are shallow-rooted. In the winter they can stand high temperatures and will grow in light or shade since they came originally from tropical jungles. The leaves of some varieties are different and decorative.

Buy a plant from a nursery, garden center, or florist. Then sucker your own new plant after flowering. See Chapter 4 on raising a pineapple plant.

A *cactus* is a strange desert plant, native to the New World, where there are over 8,000 species, ranging from enormous, tree-like plants, to tiny ones no longer than a dime. They are perennials with spine cushions, and can stand drought because their succulent stems and leaves contain water storage tissues. Many have amusing nicknames that children enjoy: bunny ears, silk pincushion, old man. Their flowers always come as a surprise. They are brilliant in color and silky in texture. Cactus plants grow best in a light mixture of leafmold, sand, and loam, with a layer of sand, not too fine, on top.

Select several varieties from the local florist, garden center, or supermarket. If they are unplanted, pot them in a shallow bowl or other container. Use gloves and tweezers when potting them and work carefully. They have very shallow roots and like to be dry, so do not over-water. Protect them from the cold. They go through a dormant period in winter and need very little water then. In the summer, however, they grow and need more moisture.

Try growing cactus from seed. It germinates easily in moist

Cactus

soil and a temperature around seventy degrees. Use a clay
pot about two inches deep. Cover the drainage hole with blobs
of cotton wool so that some of it hangs out of the hole. Fill
the pot almost to the top with the soil mixture, but do not
pack the soil down. Soak the pot until the top of the soil is
moist.

The seeds will range in size considerably, depending upon the
variety. For medium-size seeds, sprinkle them on top of the
soil and sprinkle just enough sand over them to cover them.
For larger seeds, scatter them with tweezers, then press them
lightly into the soil with a dry finger, and cover with a fine layer
of sand. They should germinate in three days to three weeks. For
the first three months water them only through the cotton. The
little plants will be very tiny and grow very slowly. Don't try to
move them too soon, because they have very small roots. Shade
the seedlings from the direct sun, but keep them where the air is
fresh.

Cactus can be propagated by cuttings. Cut them from the
narrowest point of the branching. Let the cutting dry out for
a week or so, until it is calloused over; then insert into soil or
peat-sand mixture.

Geraniums (Pelargonium) are probably America's favorite
indoor plant. They have been grown in England and America

Geranium

for more than 250 years. Perhaps the reason for this popularity is not only the generous blooming and interesting foliage, but also the ability to stand neglect. Still another reason is the wide variety available—dwarf and miniature geraniums, very dainty and less than six inches high; zonal types larger than dwarfs but not as large as the regular ones; fancy-leaved plants grown for their foliage and leaf colors; and perhaps best of all, the ones with leaves that smell like peppermint, roses, nutmeg, lemon, almond, strawberry, coconut, and ginger. Many of these, however, have unimpressive flowers.

Geraniums like full sun, daytime temperatures of seventy to seventy-five degrees, and fifty-five to sixty degrees at night. They do not like wet roots; so the soil should be kept barely moist. If they get too hot they will become leggy. They originally came from South Africa and were brought to England around 1700.

Make a project out of growing geraniums from seeds. Plant the seeds in potting soil to which some sand has been added. The tiny plants are pretty and interesting, each like a miniature grown plant.

Geraniums can get too large and leggy over the summer to carry over into the winter. Start new plants from six-inch cuttings placed in moist sand or other rooting mixure. They will take only about three weeks to root. In six to eight weeks they will be ready to pot, and will flower in two to four months. They grow so easily from cuttings that no one ever has to be without a geranium in the kitchen window.

Start a new hobby together. Grow and collect miniature geraniums, or make a collection of sweet-scented varieties.

Gloxinias are named after B. P. Gloxin, a botanist from Colmar around 1785. They were introduced from Brazil into England. The flowers come in all colors except yellow and blue. Some are marked and spotted. Notice the unusual throat markings on a gloxinia flower.

They belong to the same big family as African violets. They have fleshy, wrinkled leaves and irregularly shaped flowers, blooming sometimes alone and sometimes in clusters of hanging panicles. The flowers are usually tubular with five lobes.

When bought as plants, gloxinias often drop their flowers because of dry air and heat indoors. Try starting them from tubers. The indented side of the tuber is on top. Use a four- or five-inch pot unless the tuber is unusually large.

Gloxinias can be very fussy, so make sure that the pot is clean and has good drainage. Cover the tuber lightly with very fine soil. When growth starts give it light but not direct sun. It is tropical and originally grew under tall trees. Turn the pot to keep the plant straight. Keep it moist but not wet. Provide humidity by putting the pot inside a larger container and packing the space between with moist sphagnum moss. Set the pot on pebbles in the container so that roots will not get waterlogged.

Gloxinias can be grown from seed. Sow the seed in July for March or April flowers. Keep the pan or pot about sixty to seventy degrees warm. Cover it with glass or plastic until the seeds germinate. When they have made four leaves, transplant each to a pot, but in doing so do not let the roots be exposed. Take them up with soil around the roots. Water the seedlings the day before so that the soil will stick to the roots. Use rain water if possible.

Try raising gloxinias by leaf and stem cuttings like their cousins, the African violets.

Miniature roses are newly popular for indoor growing. Information about these miniatures came to England by way of clipper ships that carried a variety of them from Asia. They were found growing in the Alps a century ago by a Colonel Roulet, after whom that variety was named. It is still available, called *Rosa rouletti*. A variety called Tom Thumb was the first to be grown from seed.

These small plants with their tiny leaves are hardy. When they blossom, the miniature rose can have as many as sixty petals! Buy little plants from a nursery or florist, or better still, buy dormant, bare-root plants in the winter or spring and grow them yourself in pots, strawberry boxes, or other containers. They need at least three hours of sunlight a day to bloom, and will bloom in about seven weeks. Keep them in a cool room of about sixty-five degrees and provide humidity by setting the pot on pebbles in a bowl with water below the level of the pot. Fertilize the soil during the growing period.

When they bloom, set the miniature rosebushes where they may be seen closely. They are lovely little replicas of garden roses on a small-child scale. Children love them for their tiny size.

Shrimp Plant (Beloperone guttata) is a tropical plant, common in the South. It has been a popular plant for indoor gardening for a long time. Its original home was Mexico.

Buy a plant from the florist or nursery. Notice the long, overlapping segments that hang down. They look a bit like the segments of a large, cooked shrimp. The red segments that look like flowers are really bracts. Find the real flowers. They are at the end—white and rather small.

This plant likes sun and humidity. It likes a temperature of sixty-five to seventy-five degrees. Wait until the surface of the soil is dry before re-watering.

In the tropics the shrimp plant will grow up to five feet tall, but indoors it seldom reaches more than a foot and a half. If the plant gets leggy, cut it back to within four inches of the pot.

Root the cuttings in a moist root-starting mixture. Cover the cuttings with glass or plastic to conserve moisture. When the cuttings have rooted and started making leaves, transplant each

Shrimp Plant

to a pot filled with a light, sandy soil. Give them sun, humidity, and warmth, and they will soon grow to gift size.

Sultana (Impatiens) is so popular and well-known that it has many nicknames, such as Busy Lizzie, Patience, and Periwinkle. It is a constant bloomer, with flowers about an inch or so in size. They may be red, rose, salmon, pink, or white.

This plant can grow three feet tall, so ask for a dwarf variety when buying a plant from the florist or nursery. It likes sunny windows in the winter, and shade in the summer.

Grow it from seeds planted in the spring, or by rooting stem cuttings in water, moist sand, or potting soil.

CHAPTER 10

Clingers, Climbers, and Twisters: The Ivy League

Plants that climb up or hang down provide variety in indoor gardening. Whether climbing up a little trellis or hanging from a windowbox or basket, they use space not utilized by other plants.

Something To Talk About

Look at some outdoor vines. Talk about the different ways they grow and climb. Look for some with little *tendrils* that coil around string or wire. Sweetpeas have such tendrils. So do clematis and gourds.

Notice vines that have rootlike *holdfasts* along their stems, or disks at the ends of tendrils. Boston ivy, English ivy, and the trumpet vine have such holdfasts.

Some vines are *twisters*. Their stems go round and round some support. Morning glories, bittersweet, honeysuckle, and silver lace vine are all twisters.

Some have very slender stems that have to have some sort

of support. Climbing roses belong to such plants. So do jasmine, creeping lantanas, and ivy geraniums.

Learning about Supports for Vines

Talk about the best ways to support the various vines. They require something to climb on, suitable to their way of growing and strong enough to bear their weight.

One type, a totem pole, is a wooden stick about an inch and a half in diameter and about three feet long. To make, wrap thick layers of moist sphagnum moss around the stick. Hold it in place with spiralling copper wire. Two other sticks attached in a cross position to the bottom of the pole, and placed in the bottom of the pot, will hold the pole upright under the vine's weight.

A moss stick is somewhat similar. It is a cylinder of hardware cloth (quarter-inch mesh wire), twelve inches wide and three feet long. Roll it into a long cylinder, overlapping about a half-inch. Make the diameter about three and a half inches wide and fasten the seam with wire. Add crossed sticks at the bottom to help hold the cylinder in place and fill it with moist sphagnum moss, packing it tightly. It will provide not only something to cling too, but also humidity.

A large slab of bark makes a good support, often used with climbing philodendrons. Buy the slab from a florist or garden center.

Strings or wires can be strung around a window frame. A small-size trellis can be arched over a potted vine. Just make sure that the supports are sturdy. Vines can be heavy.

Florists and garden supply stores carry wire frame baskets for hanging from a hook or other support. Line the frame basket thickly with moist sphagnum moss. It will keep the soil from washing out through the basket. Hanging baskets pose some problems. They are heavy and require strong support, and dry out quickly. They are hard to water because they are high, and heavy to take down. They drip when they are too wet. They do look very pretty, though, when full of graceful vines, and provide a different eye level in a room.

Clay pots can be hung by fastening a circle of heavy wire below the rim, and attaching hanging wires to this. Hang on a heavy hook and take the pot down for watering.

A windowbox with vines hanging down from it is a pretty sight, but give some thought to its weight. It must be taken down for re-filling once in a while. A good size is three to four feet long, with a minimum of ten inches across the top and a depth of eight inches. Use rot-resistant wood such as cedar or redwood. The wood should be an inch thick. Use screws, not nails. Bore three-quarter inch holes, five inches apart, for drainage. Such boxes can be lined with metal and then filled with potted plants. In that case, put a thick layer of pebbles in the bottom for the pots to sit on so that the roots will not get waterlogged.

Something To Do

Learning about Special Indoor Vines

The best way to learn about vines is to grow them and watch as they climb, twist, twine, or trail. Learn their names and habits of growth. Some of the most popular are the following:

Blackeyed Susan (Thunbergia) is a delightful little vine with cheerful flowers in orange, yellow, or white, about an inch and a half wide. They often have very dark centers; hence the name. They like sun and are annuals, but are very pretty while they last. They are twiners.

Columnea also comes in many varieties with interesting names: Early Bird, Canary, Yellow Dragon. Its flowers are in shades of yellow and orange, and look very pretty in a hanging basket. It needs no special care and grows in average light.

English Ivy (Hedera) grows well against a totem pole, a slab of bark, or can be allowed to trail. It uses rootlike holdfasts for support. There are many varieties, all with glossy leaves. They will grow in water, or in a loose, porous soil. Keep them in a north or east window, or out of direct sun. They like a cool temperature.

Grape Ivy (Cissus rhombifolia) is a vine with three-part

Columnea

leaves. It likes some but not too much sun, and average temperature. Give it strings to climb up, and propagate new plants by rooting cuttings in water.

Indoor Oak (Nicodemia) comes from Madagascar. Its leaves look very much like young oak leaves, and it arches up into a pretty shape. Let it dry up between waterings. Feed it lightly once a month. If it makes too large a fountain shape, cut it back and re-pot it.

Jade Vine (Senecio) has very pretty, glossy leaves that are green and cream color. It will grow in the shade, but prefers light. When the stems get stringy, wind them around each other.

Indoor Oak

Kangaroo Vine (Cissus antarctica) is evergreen, with shiny leaves three or four inches long. It will climb ten feet high by tendrils. It likes sun or part shade and is grown for its handsome foliage.

Madagascar Jasmine (Stephanotis) is also an evergreen vine, with thick, oval, shiny leaves about four inches long. Its flowers are small, white, trumpet-shaped, and very fragrant. It is a twister.

Orchid Cactus (Epiphyllum) grows wild on mossy trunks of trees in tropical America. It clings to the bark of the trees by means of long, white roots, and gets its moisture from the moss and air. Its branches are pointed, jointed, and flattened. They look like leaves but are really stems.

This plant has large, beautiful, bright red, trumpet-shaped flowers with many petals several inches in diameter. They have long, white stamens. Other varieties are pink, cream, or white.

Give this plant less water in the fall while it is resting. Add more water when it starts to bud. Propagate it by cuttings from the broadest part of a stem, rooting them in moist sand and peat moss mixture. It can also be propagated by cutting off the small new stems growing from the base.

Passion Flower (Passiflora) is a fast-growing vine that can climb twenty feet or so by tendrils. It has very intricate, interesting flowers and evergreen leaves. It likes sun and can be moved outdoors to the porch or patio in the summer. In the fall take stem cuttings and root them in water for new plants.

Philodendrons can be climbers. Varieties called Red Emerald and Emerald Queen are bushy at first, then after quite a while, begin to climb by holdfasts. A slab of bark is good for them to climb on. Plant them together. One is a dark green, the other a lighter green; and they look very pretty together. They need light but will grow without sun. Water them when the soil is dry and re-pot them when they grow too large. The leaves of philodendrons will get smaller and smaller if they are not given something to climb on.

Pellionia is a creeper. Its thick, trailing leaves have net-like markings on purple stems. It likes warmth and moisture. Use it in hanging baskets. Propagate it by rooting stem cuttings in moist starting mixtures.

Wax Plant (Hoya) is an old favorite, and many varieties are available. It has glossy, thick leaves, and clusters of white, star-shaped flowers. One variety, Hindu Queen, has very curly, twisty leaves with clusters of very fragrant, creamy blossoms.

The wax plant climbs by rootlets on the stems or by twining. It will not blossom without sun, but its leaves are pretty even when it is not in bloom.

The flowers of all wax plants grow from brown knobs on the stems in the spring. Do not pick the flowers, because new flowers will grow from the same knobs the next year. The wax plant will not bloom until it is well established, and it grows very slowly.

Propagate it from stem cuttings started in a moist rooting mixture. It likes coarse soil kept on the dry side.

Train the wax plant up around a window or over an arched trellis.

CHAPTER 11

Exciting Do-togethers
for Enthusiastic
Indoor Gardeners

Indoor gardening can provide many activities not generally thought of in terms of growing houseplants or seedlings, either indoors or outdoors. These fringe activities are often excellent ways of involving the child and adult in do-together projects.

Something To Talk About

Talk about the use of outdoor plants indoors. Go out and collect flowers and boughs for indoor decoration. Look for small plants, nature's hideaways, that might thrive indoors under proper conditions. Discuss the sort of soil needed and how to give them the proper temperatures and humidity that they would get on the forest floor.

Talk about the elements of flower arranging. Select the vases and containers that might be used for bring-home flowers, cut or growing. Talk to friends and neighbors about their gardening hobbies. Keep interest in growing and caring for plants at a high level. Consult together on where plants should be placed to give the greatest pleasure to the family. Discuss which ones can be propagated to make gifts for friends.

Something To Do

Learning about Flower Arranging

Encourage the child to try his hand at it. Let him pick his own selection of flowers from the florist or the garden. Encourage originality. Talk about the possibilities of interesting arrangements in unusual containers, such as a child's mug, a woven basket, a shell, a hollow figurine, or an interesting bottle.

Discuss the need for plenty of water, not just a few inches in the bottom. Provide holders if the flowers won't stay in place.

Talk about design and balance. Work together in making an arrangement in a triangular design; a round arrangement; an L-shaped one. Try using the larger flowers at the bottom to balance the smaller ones placed higher.

Encourage making special arrangements for special occasions or for special places, such as a centerpiece for a birthday party or a small arrangement for a coffee table. Give the child the pleasure of making miniature arrangements for his friends and relatives using small flowers like pansies, violets, daisies, and other little pretties. Make a May basket for Grandmother. Send a miniature arrangement up on the tray to an invalid's room or to anyone sick in bed.

Learning about Water-rooted Arrangements

These make very simple but interesting projects for the child and adult to plan and make together. Then, when interest fades, the plants can be potted and become houseplants!

Select several stem cuttings from plants that will look pretty together. Find some that will stand erect and some that might trail down. Try to find different shades of green, and leaves of varying sizes and colors. Contrast leaf textures. Select a container that will hold these cuttings comfortably. It might be a goblet, a pretty bottle, a vase, or any other container that will hold enough water to cover the stems. Wash the container carefully, both inside and out, and rinse and dry it.

Cut the plant slips long enough for the stems to go well down in the container. Remove all leaves below the water level. Wash the stems off carefully before inserting them into the water. Then sit the container and the arrangement in the light, but not in the direct sun. Sunshine encourages the growth of algae.

When the slips have rooted they will need more food than the water will provide. Add some liquid fertilizer to the water, but make it only about a fifth of what the directions call for.

Once a month will be clean-out day. Remove the plants and wash their roots off in running water, being careful not to break them. Empty the container, wash it thoroughly inside and out, rinse it well, and dry. Fill it with fresh water and insert the plants, perhaps trying out a new arrangement with them. These water-rooted arrangements make long-lasting, pretty spots of color for a room, and they are interesting to watch because they are alive and growing.

Learning about Mini-Greenhouses

Find or buy a round or rectangular fish aquarium and turn it into a woodsy garden. Such a container is called a *terrarium*.

Part of the fun will be in going out into the woods and finding small woodland plants, stones, lichens, and twigs for possible use in creating a miniature woodland scene. Take along an old spoon, a trowel, some plastic bags, and a basket to carry home the findings. Look for a piece of mossy wood, different mosses, interestingly shaped stones and pebbles. A large one may give the effect of a stone cliff in the arrangement. Search for small woodland plants not on the conservation list— plants such as trailing cedar, Prince's pine, pipsissewa, partridge berry, and wintergreen. Dig each up carefully with the spoon or trowel, taking care to keep a small ball of the wood soil around the roots. Put each in a separate plastic bag to keep it from drying out. Collect the different mosses in separate bags, too.

When back home with the treasures, collect the planting

materials needed. Put a layer of moss around the bottom edges to conceal the soil. Then pour in a shallow layer of sand for drainage. Add about four inches of rich potting soil, arranging it so that it has interesting contours. Decide where the rocks or pebbles will look best, and arrange them accordingly. Take the little plants out of the bags and look them over for size and shape. The tallest plants will look best in the back of the container. Save the tiniest for the front so that they will be seen. Plant each one carefully, making a depression in the soil and sitting the little plant in it. Tamp the soil around it lightly with a pencil end or other small object. Add extra soil if necessary, so that every root gets covered well.

When the planting is done, use the rest of the moss to cover the soil. Add that interesting bit of branch that looks like a small, fallen log. Look at the arrangement critically and make any changes that will add to its beauty. Then water the arrangement thoroughly, using a spray if possible. Do not make it soggy. Cover the terrarium with a piece of glass to preserve warmth and moisture. If the glass gets drops of moisture on it, remove it, wipe it off, and let the plants air for a while. Touch the soil now and then and add water if it seems at all dry. It may not be necessary to water it again for several weeks.

If the plants grow too large, pinch them back. Keep the mini-greenhouse where it gets light, but out of the sun—it will cook the little plants. Rotate it to keep the plants from leaning too far over toward the light.

Try using all sorts of containers for mini-greenhouses. Apothecary jars are fine. So are glass oven dishes, glass salad bowls, goblets, brandy snifters, fingerbowls, and any open-necked glass bottle. Even one small plant in a small container can give a room a touch of the outdoors.

Learning about Bonsai

The word *bonsai* means planted in a tray. It is a process of growing a woody plant in a shallow container in harmony with the plant. In the process the plant is miniaturized. It grows, but very slowly, and is trained into an artistic shape.

Discuss which young tree seedlings will be suitable. Take a walk in woods or fields and look for a small, well-shaped hemlock, spruce, or other evergreen. Or find an attractive beech or birch tree, a ginkgo, or Japanese maple. See if a local orchard owner can let you have a very young cherry, quince, apricot, or other flowering tree. Dig up the tree with a ball of earth around its roots.

Then study the little tree. Talk about and decide which branches should be pruned off to make its shape more interesting. Decide which side will be the front of the tree.

The kind of tree should decide the type of container. An evergreen that looks as though it were shaped by high winds needs a natural, rough-looking container. A dainty little Japanese maple will look better in a lighter, daintier container.

To plant, cover the bottom of the container with a layer of sand mixed with peat moss for drainage. Use very fine potting soil mixed with humus and peat moss for the growing mixture. Shake off about a third of the soil from the little tree and cut off any roots that protrude beyond the ball of soil. Decide about the composition or design, and plant the little tree in the container to carry out the design. The tree may need some sort of support until its roots get established.

Prune the little tree. Cut back the tip of each twig to a joint, or where a leaf joins a branch. Then study its shape. Should it grow sharply to the right? Take fine copper wire and twist it lightly around the branches. Keep it loose. Do not let it cut the tender bark. Then bend the branch, a little at a time, into the wanted shape. Do the same with the trunk of the little tree, perhaps using slightly heavier wire. Do not try to get the tree into shape at one time. Work on it from week to week.

In about a year the bonsai will need to be re-potted because it will have exhausted the food supply. Prune back the roots at that time and make sure that pruning the branches keeps the tree in the right shape. The idea is to keep the tree healthy and strong—but small.

The art of bonsai goes back to the thirteenth century and is considered a great art in Japan. It has become a popular hobby in America.

Bonsai can live outdoors in a windowbox, terrace, porch, or patio in the spring, summer, and fall. Hardy varieties of trees can be mulched to go through the winter. Usually, however, the bonsai is brought indoors. Inside, it needs more humidity and more frequent watering. Do not ever let the soil dry out. Feed it like a houseplant, but use only a quarter as much fertilizer. Keep it alive but growing very slowly, keeping it small in size.

Learning about Living Christmas Trees

Instead of a throw-away tree, try buying a living tree and planting it outside in the spring. Buy the tree at least ten days before Christmas. Choose a well-shaped, well-developed one. Take it home and cover the burlapped roots with a big square of plastic. Make sure that the burlapped ball is well-watered before wrapping it. Store the tree in a sheltered place and keep it moist.

At Christmas, take the tree indoors, remove the plastic, set the burlapped roots into a container, and water it daily. After Christmas, re-cover the burlap with the plastic and store the tree in a sheltered place, such as a terrace, a garage, barn, cellar, patio, or porch until the ground is free from frost. Then plant the tree outdoors. It will be a constant reminder of a happy time.

Learning about Cut Flowers

Talk about the reason flowers should be cut on a slant: so that in water their stems will not be flat against the bottom of the vase, cutting off the stem's water supply. For flowers with very milky sap, such as poppies, poinsettias, Canterbury bells, and hollyhocks, sear the cut end at once. Figure out ways to do this. Take a cigarette lighter or a lighted candle out into the garden and sear each stem as it is cut. Or plunge the bottom of the stem into boiling water as soon as possible.

Always remove all leaves below the waterline in the vase. They will rot and smell. Condition flowers by soaking them in lukewarm water until it cools. Then arrange them.

To keep cut flowers, place them in enough water, uncrowded, out of drafts, heat, and sun. Change the water daily, and if necessary, cut another bit off the bottom stems.

Cut poinsettias make beautiful arrangements for Christmas. Add two tablespoonful of sugar to the water in the vase. Do the same every time the water is changed. The flowers will stay fresh for two weeks.

Learning How to Force Shrub and Tree Branches

On a mild day or thaw in January or February, or after a rain, go out and look for flower buds on the boughs of trees and shrubs. They will be plump, starting to swell. Pick branches of forsythia, azalea, witch hazel, pussy willow, apple trees, cherry trees, or crabapple trees. Cut the branches on a slant, just above a node, or back to the main branch. This will be a sort of pruning for the plant, so keep its shape in mind. Bring the branches indoors and pound the bottom few inches of each branch with a hammer, or slit the lower two inches of the branch with a knife. Sink the branches in a tub or bucket for a few hours. Then arrange them in a vase or bowl. They will blossom in a few weeks and bring a breath of spring to winter. Keep the room warm and give the boughs light but not direct sun.

Before throwing them out after flowering, look for roots along some of the stems. These stems can be planted to make new shrubs. Forsythia and pussy willow root very easily.

Learning To Preserve Leaves

In the fall when the leaves of some trees are brightly colored, and in the winter when fresh flowers are expensive, leaves make beautiful and interesting arrangements. Go out together in the late summer and early fall and gather branches of colored leaves. Cut some broadleaved evergreens, too, such as magnolia and rhododendron leaves. Pound the lower two inches of the stems with a hammer to allow water to penetrate the stems.

Stand the branches upright in a jar, vase, or bottle holding five inches of a mixture of one-third glycerine and two-thirds water. Do not overcrowd the boughs. Wipe each leaf with a soft cloth soaked in the mixture for quicker results.

Leave the boughs in a well-aired room and make sure that the mixture stays at five inches. It will take a few days to two weeks to get the color you want. Then remove the boughs from the mixture and arrange them in an attractive container for home decoration. The container will not need to hold water.

The leaves of branches so treated will remain soft, pliable, and satiny. Magnolia leaves will turn a bronzy brown. Green beech leaves will turn an olive color. Yellow birch leaves will turn a dark red. Forsythia leaves turn very dark.

Leaves so treated will last for years. They can be cleaned with a soft cloth and stored when not in use. They can be placed in water with fresh flower arrangements.

Individual leaves can be preserved by putting them into a pan and covering them with a mixture of half glycerine and half water.

Resources

The following listings of books and sources of seeds, bulbs, and plants represent only a few out of many. Consult the public library, local newspapers, local nurseries, and other nearby sources for close-to-home addresses.

BOOKS

Bush-Brown, Louise: *Young America's Garden Book*. New York: Scribner Pub. Co., 1962

Field, Xenia: *Growing Bulbs in the House*. New York: St. Martin's Press, 1966

Fogg, H. G. Witham: *Begonias, Gloxinias and African Violets*. London, England: John Gifford, Ltd., 1967

Free, Montague: *All About House Plants*. New York: Doubleday and Co., 1946

————: *Gardening in Containers*. Menlo Park, Cal.: Sunset Books, 1959

Harshbarger, Gretchen Fischer: *McCall's Garden Book*. New York: Simon and Schuster, 1967

Jenkins, Dorothy H.: *Encyclopedia of House Plants*. New York: Bantam Books, Inc., 1962

Langer, Richard W.: *After-Dinner Gardening Book, The.* New York: Macmillan Co., 1969

Pellegrini, Angelo M.: *Food Lover's Guide, The.* New York: Knopf Pub. Co., 1970

Peters, Ruth Marie: *Bulb Magic in Your Window.* New York: M. Barrows and Co., 1954

Schuler, Stanley: *Gardening with Ease.* New York: Macmillan Co., 1970

BULBS

Douglas Seed Co., Ltd., Brentwood, Ontario, Canada
P. De Jager and Sons, Ltd., South Hamilton, Mass. 01982
Inter-state Nurseries, Inc., Hamburg, Iowa 51640
Michigan Bulb Co., Grand Rapids, Mich. 49502
Grant Mitsch, Canby, Oreg. 97103
John Scheepers, Inc., 37 Wall St., New York, N. Y. 10005
Wayside Gardens, Mentor, Ohio 44060

HARD-TO-FIND SEEDS FOR TROPICAL AND EXOTIC PLANTS

George W. Park Seed Co., Greenwood, S. C. 29646
Harry E. Sayer, Dimondale, Mich. 48821
R. H. Shumway, Seedsman, Box 427, Rockford, Ill. 61101

INDOOR PLANTS

Alberts and Merkel Bros., Inc., P. O. Box 537, Boynton Beach, Fla. 33435
Fischer Greenhouses (African violets), Linwood, N. J. 08221
House Plant Corner (supplies), Box 810, Oxford, Md. 21654
Jackson and Perkins Co., Medford, Oreg. 97501
Johnson Cactus Gardens, Paramont, Calif. 90724
Logee's Greenhouses, 55 North St., Danielson, Conn. 06239
George W. Park Seed Co., Greenwood, S. C. 29646
Tinari Greenhouse (African violets), 2325 Valley Rd., Huntington Valley, Pa. 19006
Wilson Bros., Roachdale, Ind. 46172

SEEDS AND POTTED HERBS

W. Atlee Burpee Co., Philadelphia, Pa. 19132
Henry Field Co., Shenandoah, Iowa 51601
Jackson and Perkins Co., Medford, Oreg. 97501
Michigan Bulb Co., Grand Rapids, Mich. 49503
Tool Shed Herb Nursery, Salem Center, North Salem, N. Y. 10560
Wayside Gardens, Mentor, Ohio 44060
Weston Nurseries, East Main St., Hopkinton, Mass. 01748
White Flower Farm, Litchfield, Conn. 16759